The Winning School Bond

A Citizen's Guide to a Successful School Bond Campaign

Cheryl M. Conrod

A SCARECROWEDUCATION BOOK

The Scarecrow Press, Inc.
Lanham, Maryland, and London
2002

A SCARECROWEDUCATION BOOK

Published in the United States of America
by Scarecrow Press, Inc.
A Member of the Rowman & Littlefield Publishing Group
4720 Boston Way, Lanham, Maryland 20706
www.scarecroweducation.com

4 Pleydell Gardens, Folkestone
Kent CT20 2DN, England

British Library Cataloguing in Publication Information Available

Library of Congress Cataloging-in-Publication Data
Conrod, Cheryl M., 1948–
    The winning school bond : a citizen's guide to a successful school bond
campaign / Cheryl M. Conrod.
        p. cm.
    "A ScarecrowEducation book."
    Includes bibliographical references (p.) and index.
    ISBN 0-8108-4268-8 (paper : alk. paper)
        1. School bonds—United States. 2. School buildings—United States—
Finance. I. Title.
LB2825 .C615 2002
379.1'1—dc21   2002024028

⊗™ The paper used in this publication meets the minimum requirements of
American National Standard for Information Sciences—Permanence of Paper
for Printed Library Materials, ANSI/NISO Z39.48-1992.
Manufactured in the United States of America.

This book is dedicated to my husband Bill and my son DJ. They endured a messy house, sketchy meals, and a shortage of clean socks with good cheer while I researched and wrote this book.

I also dedicate it to my parents Joyce and George McGinley, who encouraged my every harebrained scheme and provided the education to make things happen.

Finally, I dedicate this book to members of all those school bond citizens committees who work so hard and selflessly to improve their local schools for the benefit of the children and their communities.

Contents

Preface

This book is based on one person's experiences, research, and opinions. Every school bond campaign is different, and every bit of advice offered in this book may not be suitable for every school bond initiative.

For future revisions, all comments, suggestions, criticisms, and advice will be cheerfully accepted at bcdconrod@yahoo.com.

Acknowledgments

I am deeply indebted to the many people who helped and encouraged me to write this book.

The members of the O'Neill Elementary School Needs Committee who selflessly gave so much of themselves for the good of their community: Ron Anderson, Monique Gutshall, John Hoke, Doris Price, Christina Lund, Larry Cole, Scott Haskell, Barbara Birmingham, Sue Tomjack, Cindy Somer, Laura Ahlstedt, Arthur "Bub" Tibbetts, and Sue Asher. We sometimes bickered as family, fused our unrealized talents into occasional fits of genius, and formed firm and lasting friendships.

Shari Gribble of Play it Again Productions, our video expert. She forged a key that unlocked many doors.

The Nebraska School District 7 school board members who discovered our committee on their doorstep and dove out of the way: Gary Malmberg, Dr. Robert Owens, Dr. Richard Fitch, Paul Mann, Richard Hacker, and David Spiegel.

Members of the school district administration who did all they could for us: Superintendent Doug Nollette and Secretary Carol Poese.

Principal Denis Kaeding of O'Neill Elementary School, who opened all doors, even the embarrassing ones, and the teachers and staff for their good will, sound suggestions, and hard work.

Darwin Reider of Kirkpatrick Pettis, a true veteran of many bond campaigns, with special thanks for so generously sharing his time, expertise, and advice.

James A. Dyck of The Architectural Partnership, Lincoln, Nebraska, architect and advocate for school improvement.

Brian Hale, publications director, Nebraska Association of School Boards, for encouragement, research materials, and suggestions for this project.

Ray Clark and the *Omaha World Herald*, who through the START initiative for small-town development launched us down the long hard road to a new school.

Introduction

When a man decides to do something he must go all the way, but he must take responsibility for what he does . . . No matter what he does, he must know first why he is doing it, and then he must proceed with his actions with no doubts or remorse . . .

Carlos Castaneda, *Journey to Ixtlan*

Do any of these comments sound familiar to you?

Parent: "My children have to go to a school that's unsafe, unhealthy, and unpleasant. Why don't they replace that ratty old school?"

Businessman: "I know the old relic is hurting business. I can't attract quality employees if they have school-age children. Once they hear about our school situation, young professionals with kids won't settle here."

Teacher: "Teaching in that old school is becoming intolerable. The building is crumbling around us. We're holding classes in closets. Overcrowding seems to cause more fights and discipline problems. If something isn't done soon, I'm going to start looking for a teaching position somewhere else."

Superintendent: "I don't know how we're going to get around this one. The fire marshall is on our case again for code violations. Any day we could be sued for not providing handicapped access. We could continue to put more money into the old building, but it's falling apart. It doesn't serve our modern teaching techniques and new programs. We need a new facility."

Student: "This school is the pits—drafty windows, clanking pipes, dark, tiny classrooms. It gets so stuffy in here after lunch that I'm half asleep in my afternoon classes."

School board member: "That last school bond got hammered at the polls. I don't know what went wrong. I faced recall just for trying to improve the school! If that's how people feel, I'm not about to put my neck on that chopping block again."

Senior citizen: "I live on a fixed income. I sure don't want to see my taxes go up, but that old school is a disgrace. My own children moved away to find better schools for their kids. This town will dry up and blow away if we don't do something."

Old-timer: "I went to that school when I was a kid, and I turned out all right. What was good enough for me is good enough for kids nowadays. It's the teachers, not the building, who make a school."

Citizen: "This old school is falling down. When is somebody going to do something about it?"

Do any of these comments fit your school's situation? Is school improvement badly needed? Do many people in your community believe something needs to be done?

Perhaps one or more school bond issues have gone down in flames. The community has bickered and squabbled, and everybody's angry. What to do now? Who will do it? Where do you start?

This book is a road map that can guide you to a successful school bond referendum. It will show you the most direct, efficient route. It will steer you clear of the potholes of voter apathy, distracting side issues, special situations, and opposition.

It contains a detailed plan to help you:

- Recruit and organize an effective school improvement committee
- Focus the community's attention on the school situation
- Engage the public in a thorough debate and seek consensus
- Work effectively with the school board
- Educate the citizens of the school's problems and what can be done about them
- Find school bond supporters and motivate them to vote "yes" at election time
- Through it all, maintain the emotional health of your community

COMMON REASONS WHY SCHOOL IMPROVEMENT IS NEEDED

Schools need improvement for many reasons:

- Student population has increased. You need a new or bigger school to relieve overcrowding.
- Student population has declined. It's time to join nearby towns and build a new school to serve them all.
- School facilities are outdated. Classrooms are too small. Electrical wiring is inadequate or dangerous.
- Facilities have become expensive to maintain: old plumbing, poor insulation, leaking roof, inefficient furnace.
- School buildings do not meet health, safety, or access regulations.
- School buildings must be replaced or repaired owing to flood, storm, or fire damage.
- School buildings have simply worn out.

HERE'S WHAT YOU ARE UP AGAINST

In the United States today, public school enrollment is increasing as school buildings are deteriorating. According to a 2001 report from the U.S. Department of Education, 53.1 million children entered kindergarten through 12th grade for the 2000–2001 school year, up from 46.4 million a decade ago (U.S. Department of Education, 2001).

In 2000, the General Accounting Office reported, "While enrollments are growing, the Department of Education has found that the average public school building in 1998 was 42 years old, and in 1995 we reported that about a third of the nation's public schools needed extensive repair or replacement of one or more buildings" (GAO, 2000).

"We cannot continue to apply temporary solutions to permanent, ongoing challenges," said former U.S. Secretary of Education, Richard Riley. "Many communities need to be building more schools now, to reduce overcrowding and reduce class sizes" (U.S. Department of Education, 2000).

Many schools in use today were built right after World War II. The baby boom hit the schools during a time of major economic expansion.

In the 1950s and 1960s, it took just a few speeches, an endorsement or two, and a favorable editorial in the local newspaper to pass a school bond measure. Young, upwardly mobile parents were happy to build modern new schools for their children.

These old schools are showing their age. Today it often takes a huge effort by well-organized parents, educators, and civic and business leaders to yield a winner at the ballot box. All too often it takes more than one attempt to produce school bond success.

Why?

The baby boomers are beginning to retire. Young parents who built homes near the new post-war schools have become grandparents; many live on fixed or reduced incomes. According to the 2000 census, both men and women are postponing marriage and delaying parenthood. Today's families have fewer children. The percentage of households in the United States today that have no children of school age is increasing.

This means there are more childless households that have less or no direct involvement with their local schools. It is harder to reach these voters or to interest them in the condition of the local schools.

Taxes have increased dramatically in the past several decades. Demand for tax relief grows stronger every day. A school bond election is one of the few instances when the people have a direct choice whether to raise their own taxes. In hard times (and some people believe hard times are a chronic condition), many people become very unhappy when asked for a tax increase.

Also, beginning in the late 1960s, voters began to use their votes to express their feelings on how schools should be run. The children's need for a safe, healthy, modern learning environment sometimes takes a back seat to political, racial, personal, and religious issues.

New and stricter laws now cover health, safety, and handicapped access in schools. The explosion of modern teaching aids, methods, and equipment has increased the need to upgrade outdated facilities.

But the old school is still falling down. To manage the growing school population, some districts have resorted to split sessions, year-round sessions, and Saturday school. These stop-gap measures increase stress on staff, students, parents, and buildings. The longer improvements are put off, the more expensive they will be.

The bottom line is that it has become harder to convince the voters to approve school bonds as the schools are in greater need of improvement.

Nearly every community, sooner or later, must take up the task of building a new school, expanding or upgrading an older one, or consolidating with nearby towns. The most common way (and often the only way) to fund these necessary improvements is to approve a school bond referendum.

THE SCHOOL BOND

Building a new school or improving an old one is no simple task. Putting bricks on mortar is the easy part. What can be difficult is getting the taxpayers to agree to pay for it.

A school bond referendum is a request by the district board of education to borrow money for school improvement. Most states require a simple majority vote by the district's registered voters to approve a school bond referendum. Some states require a punishing 60 percent or two-thirds margin for approval.

THE CITIZENS' COMMITTEE

For the best chance of success, a school bond project must be supported by three elements: the school board, a volunteer citizens' committee, and the people. Think of these elements as three legs of a tripod holding up a pot of bubbling stew—a school bond initiative.

The school board: This elected body alone has the legal authority to set the size of the bond and the date for the election. The board has the final word on the scope of the improvements and the design of the project. The board usually determines the need for school improvement and then organizes a citizens' committee to support it.

The citizens' committee: This group serves as a bridge between the school board and the public (taxpayers). It may start with a specific list of improvements to be made, or it may begin with only a general feeling that something needs to be done.

The committee explores school needs; probes public awareness, opinions, and wishes; builds community support for school improvement; and inspires people to vote for the bond.

The committee may be organized by the school board or it may be started by a few determined citizens. Research has shown that an active citizens' committee greatly increases the chances for a successful school bond.

The people: Also known as the voters and the taxpayers, these folks are asked to pay for the proposed school improvements. Many citizens have strong opinions about school needs and how much improvement should cost. Usually their cost estimates are low.

The people must become aware that there is a problem. They must realize that it is the whole community's problem. They must believe that the proposed solution is the best choice. They need full and honest information on what is needed and why they should support it.

The people's input is vital. If they don't believe the project reflects their feelings and opinions, they will not support it.

Each leg of the tripod is crucial. If one element is weak, the bond measure is more likely to fail.

BEFORE YOU START . . .

There are two things that have to happen before an idea catches on. One is that the idea should be good. The other is that it should fit in with the temper of the age. If it does not, even a good idea may well be passed by.

Jawaharlal Nehru, prime minister of India, 1947–1964

Consider your own situation. Is the idea good? Is there a crying need for school improvement? Can you effect school improvement with something less that would not require a school bond?

How about the "temper of the age"? Was a school board member recently involved in a major scandal? Is one or more school board members strongly opposed to school improvement?

Work to vote them out *before* mounting a school bond effort.

Has your area suffered a serious flood, a bad harvest, or a major factory closure? Have state taxes shot through the roof this year? Has the school district recently reorganized?

You might have to wait for the dust to settle before launching the school effort.

Nothing can stop a good idea whose time has come. But if the time is not right, even the best idea will fail.

The most common argument against a school bond is, "Taxes are too high already. We can't afford it." *This argument by itself is not a good enough excuse to abandon a school bond attempt.*

HOW TO USE THIS BOOK

This book will guide a citizens' group from a vague idea to a successful school bond election. There is something in it for communities of every size, but it is particularly useful for volunteer groups in small cities and towns who must go it alone without professional help or a large budget.

Read the whole book before you start. After you've read it through, the process should make more sense—what happens when and why.

You will find many more suggestions, ideas, and techniques than any one city or town should expect to tackle. Don't feel you have to try them all. Pick out and concentrate on the ones that will best suit you and your community.

Feel free to stray from the organization, techniques, or timetable laid out in the following chapters. No two school bond efforts are alike. Each community has a different set of problems, needs, and mix of citizens. Even between elections in the same town, the situation can change.

But bear in mind that all school bond campaigns are political campaigns. There are basic parallels and similar questions, issues, and techniques. The principles are the same for large cities or small towns and for massive bond issues or for tiny ones.

Two other important details about this book must be mentioned:

First, it carefully avoids use of military or warlike words or phrases, such as "weapons in your arsenal," "battle plan," or "counterattack."

Why?

Because all the people on both sides of a school bond issue are your neighbors, coworkers, and friends. If you go to war for a new school, it becomes a civil war. All the casualties will be local, painful, and slow to heal.

Second, for simplicity's sake, the generic words "his," "he," and "him" are used exclusively throughout this book. Gender has nothing to do with school bonds. Not one of the committee's tasks is restricted to men only. Women, please don't be offended.

THE ROAD AHEAD

The road to a successful school bond can be long and rough. Success will usually come only as the result of firm resolve, sharp planning, and hard work. Plan to give up a fair amount of time in pursuit of improving your school(s).

During this journey you will make close friends and a few enemies. You will find support and friendship unlooked for. You will be betrayed. You will feel hurt, anger, disappointment, exhaustion, surprise, excitement, and joy. You will learn how your community works and who are the major players. Sweet and sour, you will learn a vast amount about human nature.

You will discover, to your surprise and delight, how a small group of determined people, if they are organized and focused, can make an enormous difference for the children and for the community.

1

The Committee

Never one thing and seldom one person can make for a success. It takes a number of them merging into one perfect whole.

Marie Dressler, Canadian actress, 1869–1934

The formal decision to launch a school bond will always rest with members of the school district board of education. They are the elected officials. They have the authority, and they control the purse strings for public education.

There are three basic ways school bonds are brought before the people for a vote.

1. The school board decides what school improvement is needed. It decides on the scope of the project (often with the help of an architect) and sets the bond amount and the date for the election.
2. The school board designs the plan. After all the planning is done, the board recruits a citizens' committee to help out with the campaign.
3. The school board teams up with a citizens' committee. They work together from the beginning to develop a plan and work with the public to pass the bond.

The school board chooses the first alternative at its peril. Unless the need for school improvement is very obvious (the school has burned down) and the school board is very popular, the board will need the help of a citizens' group to educate and convince the community of the need for school improvement.

The second choice is better, but the third option will yield the best results on election day.

A citizens' committee that is involved in the earliest stages of the planning process will be the most effective. It explores the people's opinions, and it learns how much people will be willing to spend for school improvement. It can help the school board determine the scope of the project and draw up a design within the people's price range.

When and how the citizens' committee forms depends on the makeup of the school board. The board most often initiates the process by asking for volunteers to work on the committee. If school conditions are bad enough, but the school board is reluctant to start the school bond process, a citizens' committee may form on its own.

THE COMMITTEE'S TASKS

The citizens' committee will have five tasks:

1. *To open a conversation with the public.* The committee asks people if they believe improvement is needed and gathers suggestions on what that improvement might be.
2. *To educate the community on the need for school improvement.* The committee, as citizen advocates, can take the message to the community without the political baggage school board members may carry.
3. *To actively campaign for the bond issue.* A committee has a much freer hand than the school board to campaign for school bond approval. It can raise funds and spend them to sway public opinion.
4. *To make sure the "yes" votes are actually cast.* A committee, through voter identification and encouragement, gets school bond supporters to the polls.
5. *To leave the community's emotional health intact.* Through truthful, friendly, open interaction with the community, the committee avoids generating ill will that can scar school bond campaigns.

Grassroots activism is very effective. By actively and fully involving the community in the debate from the very beginning, the public will be much more likely to support school improvement.

FORMING THE COMMITTEE

In most situations, the school board will get the school improvement bandwagon rolling. If you hear its siren call, jump on.

If the school board does not set the wagon in motion, but the need for school improvement is great, you can start your own citizens' committee. As few as two citizens can take the first crucial step.

No degrees, experience, or fancy resumés are required. The only qualification for the job is the earnest opinion that something needs to be done about the old school. No doubt there are many people out there who feel the same way. They're just waiting for someone to set the process in motion.

Start by talking up school improvement among teachers and parent-teacher organization members in the affected school(s). Spread the word to friends, acquaintances, members of service clubs, and business, political, and religious leaders.

If support seems strong, call a committee-forming meeting. Set a date, time, and location that will be as convenient as possible to the most people. Send out press releases to the local newspaper and public service announcements to local radio stations. Post notices of the meeting in public places (see chapter 5, Publicity). Heavily target those neighborhoods that send kids to the school(s) in question. Invite everyone interested in improving the school situation.

The call to form a committee to look at school issues must reach the entire community. It is very important that no one be given any reason to think he is being left out. Everyone must be made to feel welcome to join.

At least two people should conduct this meeting. One will lead the discussion, the other will keep detailed notes of the comments and ideas.

To keep the meeting on track, it should be structured around an agenda. Always keep in mind the purpose of the meeting—to form a committee for school facilities improvement. This does not include gripes about individual teachers, administrators, or curriculum. Announce the purpose of the meeting at the beginning. If the discussion starts to stray from the stated agenda, firmly bring it back on track. Allow plenty of time for open discussion, but keep it focused. (For more detailed information on how to conduct meetings, see chapter 7, Ambassadors Club.)

At the meeting you will poll people:

- What are the current problems with the school facilities?
- What are possible improvements (new school, addition, upgrade, renovation, safety or access, new gym/art center/auditorium)?
- Is the location of the school important?
- What other issues concern the school buildings?

One vital task at this meeting will be to pass around a sign-up sheet. Ask everyone even remotely interested in helping out on a school improvement effort to write his name and telephone number. Reassure people there will be plenty of work for everyone, but no one will be asked to do more than his personal time or energy will allow.

This precious list contains the seeds from which you will grow the committee and the school bond effort.

What happens if turnout for the meeting is light, even though you know support is out there and the need for school improvement is great?

It's time to go hunting. Where do you find people to help? Start with the obvious people: school teachers, staff, and parents of school-age children. Seek out civic leaders, such as library, parent-teacher organization, and hospital board members. Look for prominent business, professional, and religious leaders.

Remember the old saying that is sad but true, "If you want to get something done, ask a busy person to do it." Don't be afraid to ask those busy people to join. The worst that can happen is that they will decline.

WHO SHOULD BE ON THE COMMITTEE?

The better represented all segments of the community are, the more credible the committee will be. Ideally, committee members will be assorted, interesting, and sometimes unlikely.

Not only does this quell accusations of elitism, but a well-rounded, well-connected committee taps wide-ranging talent.

Look for members with a good mix of backgrounds, occupations, ages, and interests. You want business people, seniors, homemakers, clergy, professionals and working class men and women, parents, people with no children or grown children, newcomers and old-timers, and high school and college students. You want a good religious, educational, and racial mixture, especially in districts shared with parochial schools and large ethnic populations.

Leave no stone unturned, no talent untapped.

The next step is to call everyone on the list and anyone else you've flushed out in your talent search and invite them to the next meeting—the one where the committee is formed.

THE FIRST COMMITTEE MEETING

The first committee meeting is extremely important. It sets the tone for the entire effort.

Begin the meeting by preparing potential committee members for the long haul. Make it clear that the journey will be a marathon, not a sprint. Reassure people that every effort will be made to distribute the workload evenly so no one member becomes overloaded. Advise members to pace themselves and not to be afraid to ask others for help.

Firmly set the tone for the task ahead. The committee must be prepared to always keep cool in the face of adversity. You will be entering the public arena. Some people will be unhappy with your efforts. Be ready to deal calmly with whatever nastiness you may hear on the street, on your answering machines, or in your e-mail box.

CHOOSING YOUR LEADERSHIP

Selecting your leaders is probably the most important thing you will do. *Choose carefully!* Everything that follows flows from these leaders. They are the face the committee shows to the community. They are the ones who will keep the committee focused, committed, and moving forward. If you choose well, everything moves along more smoothly. Poor choices can lead to no end of trouble.

Choose leaders who are honest, energetic, articulate, committed, and dependable and who have superb "people" skills. Your journey must be sweet and light, positive, and enthusiastic. Make sure your leaders are a good match to this theme.

Avoid at all costs leaders who are annoying, uncompromising, pushy, or mean-spirited. Many a school bond voyage has been wrecked on the rocks of personality.

THE COMMITTEE STRUCTURE

Try to build the committee structure around the talent you have on hand. Avoid squeezing your talent into a rigid framework. The committee must follow ability. Place your most able, dependable members in the most demanding positions.

First select two chairmen. Why two? Unless one person has extraordinary stamina and tons of spare time, leading the bond effort is more than one person can handle. Each chairman's work will be equivalent to a part-time job. The two chairmen should each head a subcommittee in which they feel most comfortable or have the most knowledge.

Below is a suggested organization chart; however, there are many ways to organize. If you find a more workable way, go with it.

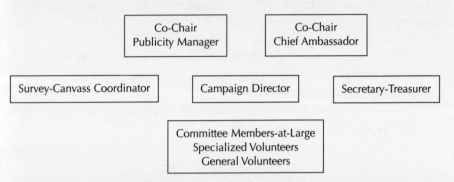

Members or volunteers with a specialty can be called on to help with specific projects, such as producing a video, designing the campaign brochure, or fund raising. General volunteers will be activated as needed for research, surveying, canvassing, and campaign work.

However you organize, it is important that duties be assigned early to each position and stuck to carefully. This will avoid confusion and conflict and will keep open the vital lines of communication.

Remember, the committee's membership is not set in stone. Members will start new jobs, move away, lose interest, or run out of time. If a subcommittee head doesn't work out, don't hesitate to transfer or replace him. Be gentle and diplomatic if you must remove someone from a leadership position. Always remember, committee members are only human. Besides, it can do irreparable harm to make an opponent out of a former committee member. The last thing you want to do is to create enemies.

You all have real lives separate for the school issue. Members must be easy on those who can't spend as much time on the effort as others. Every little bit helps.

As the committee's work gets underway, people will learn of your effort and may wish to sign on. Eagerly welcome new members. You're going to need all the help you can get.

A brief job description of your five assigned committee members follows.

Publicity Manager

This person holds one of the two most demanding positions. His is the official voice of the committee. His task is to explain who the committee is, what it plans to do, what it is doing, and what it has done. He informs, educates, and eventually convinces the community of the need for school improvement through the school bond. He coordinates all the committee's publicity efforts, which may include the following:

- To write and distribute columns, articles, editorials, and news releases for local newspapers, radio, television, and cyberspace
- To edit a newsletter
- To compile and update focus group briefing book materials, video production, or audiovisual presentation materials
- To produce campaign brochures and other literature

The publicity manager is the central switchboard for the latest news, rumors, and misinformation and responds to them in a timely manner.

This person must be good with words, cool under pressure, able to meet tight deadlines, and never suffer from writer's block. (See chapter 5, Publicity.)

Chief Ambassador

This is the other most demanding position. The chief ambassador is the eyes and ears and the face of the committee. He will take the school bond effort directly to the people through a series of focus group meetings.

He trains and schedules members of the ambassadors club to speak to community groups, clubs, employees, and gatherings. He finds the answers to questions and maintains close contact with the school board.

This person must be a good public speaker, well organized, pleasant, flexible, quick on his feet, and a great salesman. (See chapter 7, Ambassadors Club.)

Survey-Canvass Coordinator

This is the "bookends" position, covering tasks that come first and last in the school bond effort. As survey coordinator, he coordinates a community survey to find out how the citizens feel about the school situation (see chapter 3, Surveying the Community).

As canvass coordinator, he coordinates a canvass held just before election day to identify the "yes" votes (see chapter 12, The Canvass). The canvass coordinator will work on election day with the campaign director to make sure those supporters get to the polls (see chapter 13, Election Day).

Campaign Director

The official campaign lasts only three to four weeks, but there is much work to be done ahead of time. The director sees to it that the community is made thoroughly aware of the upcoming election. He works to get those "yes" votes to the polls. His duties are to:

- Coordinate fund raising activities
- Organize committee participation in community events
- Seek endorsements of prominent citizens and leaders
- Design, produce, and distribute bumper stickers, posters, and campaign buttons or ribbons
- Set up poll watching
- Organize a transportation pool to provide voters with baby-sitters or rides to the polls
- Direct a phone bank on election day to get out the vote

The campaign director must be able to handle several tasks at once under pressure. He must be good at ordering people around in such a way that they won't become offended (see chapter 11, The Campaign).

Secretary-Treasurer

The secretary-treasurer takes minutes at every meeting and provides copies to all committee members. He revises and updates the action plan as needed (see chapter 2, Planning for Success).

He maintains the committee's bank account and keeps the committee's funds on the legal side of current campaign finance regulations. He files the necessary forms during the campaign and after the election (see chapter 10, Fund Raising).

The secretary-treasurer maintains the all-important master list of supporters. As committee members identify citizens who can be counted on to vote "yes" for a school bond, the secretary-treasurer posts and updates this list throughout the entire effort.

The secretary-treasurer is the keeper of the records. He researches past school bond attempts. He interviews veterans of previous school bond efforts, both successful and failed (see chapter 4, Research).

He collects all literature, ideas, plans, and records related to past and present school bonds. After the election, he compiles a scrapbook to serve as a guidebook for future committees (see chapter 14, After the Election).

These five leaders steer and pace the project, but you cannot be successful with only five core members. The committee should have at least five more members-at-large for backup and support. Also you will need a horde of volunteers.

Members-at-Large

Unassigned members must be ready to pitch in when extra help is needed on a hot project. They must be willing to fill in when a leader is overwhelmed or away. They will take on special tasks as needed, tapping their special talents and expertise.

For example, a lawyer may provide information on campaign finance law. A writer might write columns, press releases, and briefing (focus group) materials. A graphic artist might create a logo, campaign posters, or cartoons. A computer expert might create and maintain a committee web site.

Unless one suffers from terminal stage fright, all members should be willing to conduct focus group meetings through the ambassadors club and to carry out campaign tasks.

You will be surprised at the hidden talent in the committee. Members will undoubtedly surprise themselves.

Volunteers

In addition, you will need dozens of volunteers. Specialized volunteers might include someone knowledgeable in web page design, an audiovisual technician, a journalist, an attorney, and an accountant, just to name a few. General volunteers are those willing and able to help out with big tasks such as the survey, the campaign, and the canvass. They will distribute campaign literature, hang posters, and help out at community events.

Remain constantly on the lookout to increase your volunteer pool. You can never recruit too many. Some will be good for one task but not others. Some will become disillusioned or tired of the work; others will move away. The route to a successful school bond is long and hard. The more people available to spread out the effort, the better.

TAKING THE PLEDGE

Setting up the committee's organizational structure and choosing leadership might seem to be enough effort for one session, but you're not done yet. You must set the charter, tone, and ground rules for the task before you.

What is your goal? Make sure everyone has started down the same road headed in the same direction.

Remember your five tasks:

1. To discover what school improvement is needed and gauge community interest and support (unless the school board has already decided on the amount and scope of the project)
2. To educate the community on the need for school improvement
3. To actively campaign for passage of the bond issue
4. To make sure all supporters actually cast their votes
5. To leave the community's emotional health intact

This may sound corny, but once you join this committee, you are leaving your personal self behind and becoming a "public person." You have taken on a task larger than yourself. Your personal interests must be put aside in favor of your public duty.

All committee members must pledge to conduct the upcoming community conversation in the most friendly, open, trustworthy manner possible.

Count on your project to bring out the worst in some members of the community. School bond proposals inevitably provoke strong feelings that can long outlast the bond issue. Never let your efforts bring out the worst in yourselves.

You must vow to *never* answer mean personal remarks or attacks in kind. You must agree to stick together as a group and to embrace the spirit of compromise.

It is absolutely crucial to your success that all committee members honor the pledge.

COMMITTEE MEETINGS

Prepare to meet at least twice a month; once a week would be preferable. Set a regular meeting time at an agreeable place. You might meet at a local café for lunch or spend an evening in the public library meeting room.

Why so often?

Frequent meetings are necessary to mold the committee into a solid unit, to keep up your momentum, and to maintain a strong line of communication.

Important: Invite the entire community to attend every committee meeting. Do this every time, without fail. Your door must be open always to everyone. Even if they don't come, people will be comforted knowing they are welcome and you are hiding nothing.

The co-chairs should conduct businesslike meetings from a prepared agenda. Take minutes at every meeting.

Why so rigid? Even with the best of intentions, it is easy in our workaday lives to forget what we've promised to do. The committee must depend on each member to complete assigned tasks. A prepared agenda saves time and keeps the committee focused and on track. Minutes serve as important reminders and as a means of checking progress.

THE COMMITTEE AND THE SCHOOL BOARD

The committee's relationship with the school board depends on your district's situation. Ideally, you will work in tandem and in harmony with the board, but sometimes this will not be the case. Some school boards will be enthusiastic and helpful. Others may be suspicious of a group of citizens who have taken the initiative. The worst case is if the school board ignores or resists the obvious need for improvement.

Resistance by the school board might be caused by fear of losing control or sharing power with a citizens' group. Board members may fear losing a personal election or facing a recall initiative. The board may be hesitant to launch a bond campaign after a crushing defeat or in the face of opposition by a noisy minority. Board members may have an innate fear of change.

Remember, school board members are your neighbors, colleagues, and friends. Except for getting themselves elected, they may have no more experience than your committee in running a political campaign.

One way to overcome school board reluctance is by presenting the board with a community mandate. This can be done through your initial community survey (see chapter 3, Surveying the Community).

If no argument or demonstration of dire need can move certain school board members, a last resort might have to be to wait until the next election and work to vote them out of office.

Whether the committee develops a close or detached relationship with the board depends on how the community feels about the school board. In this country, it is not uncommon for voters to mistrust our public officials. We elect them, then we criticize them. Some school boards are very unpopular, but even a popular or neutral school board carries some negative baggage.

Conversely, popular board members may also be major community leaders. They can gather strong support for school improvement.

It is up to the committee to decide if close ties between the committee and the school board will help or hurt your cause. If there is strong community resentment toward the school board, it might be a good idea for the committee to keep its distance.

In any case, keep your independence from the board. Accusations that the citizens' committee is the lap dog of the school board can be very damaging.

This doesn't mean the committee and the school board go their separate ways. The committee will work with the school board but not for it. Each has a vital role to play. There will be plenty of glory to go around when the school bond referendum has been approved.

Develop a direct, open line of communication with the school board and the school superintendent from the outset. You will need one another to get the job done. Be businesslike and flexible. This is no time for a power struggle. All must keep their eyes fixed on the prize.

At least one (and preferably more) school board member should regularly attend committee meetings. This board member will provide accurate policy information to the committee and prevent confusion.

The committee will present concise, well-organized reports to the school board at its regular meetings. This is an excellent opportunity to let the community know of your progress, because the school board proceedings are covered by the media.

Once the bond process begins, the school board should maintain a low profile. The committee should make all the presentations, asking the board and superintendent only for technical support.

The citizens' committee will have more impact in the community. It can be more effective in gathering information and support. Its hand is freer to advocate.

Board members, however, should make no secret of their support of the project. As mentioned in the introduction, the school board's support for the school bond must be unanimous. Anything less drives a wedge into your efforts and fuels the opposition's argument that there is nothing wrong with the status quo or that there is something wrong with the plan.

Remember, the committee and the school board are right and left hands, working together to improve your schools. Each hand must know what the other is doing.

The committee has formed, your leaders have been selected, the meeting place and times are set . . .

It's time to begin to map your journey.

2

Planning for Success

When the ancients said a work well begun was half done, they meant to impress the importance of always endeavoring to make a good beginning.

Polybius, Greek historian, second century BC

IT'S TIME TO BEGIN

It is much easier to take a trip if you decide in advance where you're going. Which route will you take? Who will help you along the way? How will you avoid time-consuming detours and dead ends? When do you expect to arrive?

On your journey to a successful school bond, you will need to bring order to the chaos of countless chores and details. You will need a map and an itinerary.

You will need a plan.

Through planning, the committee decides what needs to be done. You work out which tasks are most important. You decide how to tackle each job and who is the best person(s) to do it.

An action plan ensures that all the major aspects of your effort are written down, understood, and supported by all involved. A time limit or deadline for each item discourages putting things off or forgetting about them altogether.

The journey to a successful school bond can be divided into three distinct phases. By planning around these three phases, you will travel along the right road in the right direction.

THE THREE PHASES OF A SCHOOL BOND INITIATIVE

Phase I: Information

During the information phase, the committee opens a friendly conversation with the citizens of the school district. How do people feel about the school's current situation? Do they think change is needed? If so, what kind? If not, why not? How much are they willing to spend?

This phase is very neutral. The committee probes the public's attitudes but does not express any opinions of its own or suggest any course of action.

A committee-sponsored community survey is an excellent way to gauge support for school improvement (see chapter 3, Surveying the Community). Another method is to conduct focus group meetings (see chapter 7, Ambassadors Club).

The committee opens a line of communication with the school board by attending all board meetings and making monthly reports to the board. The committee forwards citizens' feelings and suggestions concerning the school situation to the board and passes along information from the board to the people.

This is also the time to study past bond attempts, both local and in other communities (see chapter 4, Research).

If, after this first phase, you find you are not sure the project is needed, or if some temporary obstacle lies between the community and school improvement, put it aside until the stars are better aligned.

If you have uncovered *strong* community support for school improvement, you begin . . .

Phase II: Education

Through your research, you've discovered major shortcomings in the current school situation. Many people are aware that something must be done, but each person you talk to has a different opinion on what that something should be. The committee's task during the education phase is to make everyone who will listen aware of the deficiencies of the school—why improvement is needed.

The committee discusses school improvement with the community through focus group meetings (chapter 7, Ambassadors Club), newspaper columns, a newsletter, committee web page, and community activities (see chapter 5, Publicity).

The committee continues its role as liaison between the public and the school board.

This is the consensus-seeking stage. The committee makes no secret of its view that improvement is needed but shows no preference for any particular plan or project.

Be careful not to start pushing too soon for a school bond initiative. If you try to sell something to people before they have had a chance to examine it, they will become suspicious of your motives. A bond levy at this stage is only one of many options available.

Until the school board has decided on a particular plan or design, strict neutrality will protect you from charges of having ulterior motives or of being a pawn of the school board.

Phase III: The Campaign

This is the shortest, most intense phase. The campaign lasts only three to four weeks, but preparing for it will take quite a bit longer.

The school board (using, one hopes, committee and citizen input) has proposed a school bond referendum, set the bond asking amount, and announced election day.

During this phase the committee becomes a strong advocate for the specific plan proposed by the school board. The committee's task during this phase is to identify supporters and motivate them to go to the polls and vote "yes" for the school bond.

THE ACTION PLAN

As you begin to list all the tasks to be completed before election day, they will seem to be a huge wall blocking your way. But if you divide up those tasks into manageable pieces, each becomes a stepping-stone leading to a successful school bond election.

An action plan keeps your tasks before you. What has to be done? When and in what order will each job be tackled? Who will do it? How much will it cost?

An action plan divides and distributes the many chores among many helping hands. Checking your progress on the plan will be the basis of your weekly committee meeting agendas.

As with the committee structure, your plan will not be carved in stone. Dates and deadlines will shift. Chores will take more time than estimated. Tasks will be added and dropped. At first no election date will be available; you will begin your trip without an arrival time.

Computerize your plan if possible. This allows for easy modification and reprinting. Keep it up-to-date and legible. If spreadsheet or word processing software is not available, be sure to write in pencil.

A sample action plan is provided as a guide. Each category or subject should have its own worksheet. List what the task is, who is in charge, when it should be completed, who can help or how it can be accomplished, and how much it should cost. Each task must have a deadline, and keep in mind that some tasks are dependent on others. Set realistic deadlines that allow for unforeseen circumstances.

Each job must have someone listed as the taskmaster, even if that person will not be doing the actual work. This person will coordinate the work, keep it on track, and work with other taskmasters on projects related to his.

The format shown in the sample is certainly not the only way to map out your journey. Your plan may be more detailed or streamlined to fit your unique situation and group. You may add chores essential to your journey or leave others out.

Here are three tips for working out your action plan. As you fill in your activities:

- Work backward from known deadlines.
- Allow roughly twice as much time as you think will be necessary.
- When you estimate your costs, under "Resources Needed," assume that expenses will overrun initial estimates.

ACTION PLANNING WORKSHEET

Objective: Research

Activity #1: Study and copy newspaper archives of previous school bond attempts.
In Charge: Secretary-treasurer
When: (deadline)
Resources Needed: Names of prominent supporters and opponents. Study mistakes, good ideas, public events, and publicity.
$:

Activity #2: Interview leaders of previous school bond campaigns.
In Charge: Secretary-treasurer
When: ASAP (deadline)
Resources Needed: Committee members
$:

Activity #3: Interview prominent opponents.
In Charge: Secretary-treasurer
When: ASAP, but when convenient and opportune
Resources Needed: Preferably committee members familiar with them
$:

Activity #4: Collect copies of campaign literature from previous school bond attempts—local, regional, state, and national.
In Charge: Secretary-treasurer (publicity manager)
When: Ongoing
Resources Needed: All committee members and volunteers
$:

Activity #5: Track down and contact college students and potential absentee voters.
In Charge: Secretary-treasurer
When: Research ongoing. Contact students at beginning of campaign phase.
Resources Needed: Committee members/volunteers
$:

Activity #6: Build and maintain list of supporters.
In Charge: Secretary-treasurer
When: Ongoing
Resources Needed: Everyone brings names to the master list.
$:

ACTION PLANNING WORKSHEET

Objective: Survey

Activity #1: Decide survey questions.
In Charge: Survey coordinator
When: (set meeting date or deadline)
Resources Needed: Input—suggestions from all committee members
$:

Activity #2: Design and print survey form.
In Charge: Survey coordinator and publicity manager
When: (set deadline)
Resources Needed: Typewriter or word processor and copier
$:

Activity #3: Announce upcoming survey.
In Charge: Publicity manager

When: (set deadline)
Resources Needed: Public service announcements and news releases
$:

Activity #4: Obtain registered voters list.
In Charge: Survey coordinator
When: (set deadline)
Resources Needed: Registrar of voters or county clerk
$:

Activity #5: Divide and distribute registered voters list and survey. Provide instructions on how to conduct survey. Rehearse.
In Charge: Survey coordinator
When: (set meeting date)
Resources Needed: Committee members and volunteers
$:

Activity #6: Conduct survey.
In Charge: Survey coordinator
When: Deadline for completion: ten days to two weeks after survey begins
Resources Needed: Survey forms, callers, and telephones
$:

Activity #7: Compile and analyze survey results. Decide whether to continue or disband committee.
In Charge: Survey coordinator
When: Set date ASAP after survey deadline.
Resources Needed: All committee members. Computer is very helpful.
$:

Activity #8: Report findings to school board and public.
In Charge: Survey coordinator and publicity manager
When: Next scheduled board meeting or letter to school board and superintendent; news release to public the following day
Resources Needed: Letters, public service announcements for radio/TV, and news releases for newspaper
$:

ACTION PLANNING WORKSHEET

Objective: Publicity

Activity #1: Choose committee name, color(s), design, and logo.
In Charge: Publicity manager
When: Education phase

Resources Needed: All committee members' input

$:

Activity #2: Briefing book (also see Focus Group Presentations [Ambassadors Club] worksheet)

In Charge: Publicity manager and chief ambassador

When: ASAP, in time for focus group meetings. Update as needed

Resources Needed: All information on past bond levies and current proposal and data from school board

$:

Activity #3: Handouts

In Charge: Publicity manager and chief ambassador

When: As needed for focus group and other meetings

Resources Needed: Data from school board, responses to focus group questions, concerns

$:

Activity #4: Newspaper column

In Charge: Publicity manager

When: Committee and newspaper(s) decide interval

Resources Needed: Members to write columns and/or to suggest topics, to proofread, and to critique columns before publication

$:

Activity #5: Video (see also video worksheet on p. 20)

In Charge: Publicity manager

When: Directly after survey, to be used in phase II and phase III

Resources Needed: Script, shooting schedule, camera, support of school administration, teachers

$:

Activity #6: Newsletter

In Charge: Publicity manager

When: Ongoing. Committee decides interval

Resources Needed: Input from all members, volunteers, and community supporters; computer or typewriter

$:

Activity #7: Web site

In Charge: Publicity manager

When: Ongoing

Resources Needed: Input from all members, volunteers, and community supporters; webmaster

$:

Activity #8: Brochure

In Charge: Publicity manager

When: Campaign phase

Resources Needed: Computer with desktop publishing software or paste pot, information from school board/superintendent, printing company or copy machine. Distribute through canvass, mail, supporting businesses, and focus group meetings.

$:

Activity #9: News releases and public service announcements for radio, TV, and newspapers

In Charge: Publicity manager

When: Continuous, as needed

Resources Needed: Input from committee members

$:

Activity #10: Public events

In Charge: Campaign director

When: Specify as events approach

Resources Needed: Specify committee members and chores.

$:

Activity #11: Collect myths, misinformation, and false rumors.

In Charge: Chief ambassador and publicity manager

When: Continuous

Resources Needed: All members and supporters listen for rumors and misinformation; will be addressed continuously in focus group meetings and in the media

$:

ACTION PLANNING WORKSHEET

Objective: Video

(If you prefer a slide show to an audiovisual presentation, substitute slides for video. Preparation is roughly the same.)

Activity #1: Contact superintendent and principal(s). Tour school with principal. Ask him to set up meetings with teachers in affected school(s).

In Charge: Publicity manager (video subcommittee)

When: Set date(s)

Resources Needed: Two committee members: one to interview, one to record

$:

Activity #2: Meeting(s) with teachers, parents, school staff
In Charge: Publicity manager (video subcommittee)
When: Specific date(s)
Resources Needed: Ask all to list problems and shortcomings of school(s) and request their assistance in filming.
$:

Activity #3: Write draft script.
In Charge: Publicity manager (video subcommittee)
When: Specific deadline
Resources Needed: Writers and editor for script
$:

Activity #4: Develop shooting schedule; notify principal/teachers.
In Charge: Publicity manager
When: Specific date
Resources Needed: Cooperation of administration, faculty, and students
$:

Activity #5: Shoot video.
In Charge: Publicity manager (video subcommittee)
When: Specific date
Resources Needed: Camera, cameraman, director, narrator, cooperation of teachers, students
$:

Activity #6: Edit and narrate video.
In Charge: Publicity manager (video subcommittee)
When: Specific date
Resources Needed: Video subcommittee members, draft script, approval of committee and school board
$:

Activity #7: Copy video and distribute it for focus group use.
In Charge: Publicity manager (video subcommittee)
When: ASAP
Resources Needed: Ambassadors, video player, monitor or slide projector and screen
$:

ACTION PLANNING WORKSHEET

Objective: Focus Group Presentations (Ambassadors Club)

Activity #1: Compile list of all community groups.
In Charge: Chief ambassador

When: Ongoing
Resources Needed: All committee members gather names of groups.
$:

Activity #2: Coordinate and schedule focus group meetings.
In Charge: Chief ambassador
When: Ongoing
Resources Needed: Each member chooses groups with which he is affiliated/familiar. Divide others up equally. Revisit groups already contacted as more information becomes available.
$:

Activity #3: Focus group meeting rehearsal
In Charge: Chief ambassador
When: Before first focus group meeting
Resources Needed: All ambassadors
$:

Activity #4: Briefing book
In Charge: Chief ambassador and publicity manager
When: ASAP before first focus group meetings. Update as needed.
Resources Needed: Pro/con sheets, history of past bond issues, historic photos, current fact sheets. Add proposed school design and financial information as it becomes available.
$:

Activity #5: Compile list of names and numbers of supporters collected during each focus group meeting.
In Charge: Focus group leader and secretary-treasurer
When: At each focus group meeting
Resources Needed: Secretary-treasurer keeps master list of identified supporters and volunteers.
$:

ACTION PLANNING WORKSHEET

Objective: Fund Raising

Activity #1: Open checking account.
In Charge: Secretary-treasurer
When: Directly after committee is formed
Resources Needed: Knowledge of regulations regarding campaign finance reporting
$:

Activity #2: Solicit funds from service organizations, business, civic groups, etc.
In Charge: Secretary-treasurer
When: Ongoing during education and campaign phases
Resources Needed: Committee members and volunteers
$:

Activity #3: Plan fund raising activities.
In Charge: Secretary-treasurer, publicity manager, and campaign director
When: Ongoing
Resources Needed: All committee members, supporters, and volunteers
$:

Activity #4: Plan activities for community celebrations.
In Charge: Publicity manager and campaign director
When: Ongoing
Resources Needed: All committee members. Entertain any and all suggestions.
$:

Activity #5: Log all $$ activity.
In Charge: Secretary-treasurer
When: Ongoing
Resources Needed: Spreadsheet, legal advice (nonprofit tax number)
$:

Activity #6: File campaign finance reports.
In Charge: Secretary-treasurer
When: As required by law
Resources Needed: Ledger, records, proper forms, legal advice
$:

ACTION PLANNING WORKSHEET

Objective: Campaign

Activity #1: Choose campaign slogan.
In Charge: Campaign director and publicity manager
When: Start of campaign
Resources Needed: All committee members
$:

Activity #2: Voter registration of out-of-town students and supporters
In Charge: Campaign director

When: Deadline for completion: last day of voter registration

Resources Needed: List of college students, other supporters, cover letter, registration forms, and absentee request forms

$:

Activity #3: Voter registration—local

In Charge: Campaign director and publicity manager

When: One week before registration deadline

Resources Needed: Set up booth and advertise. Get list of unregistered supporters and local high school students of voting age.

$:

Activity #4: Buy or make campaign tokens and premiums.

In Charge: Campaign director

When: To be ready for campaign phase

Resources Needed: Committee members, volunteers, and supporters

$:

Activity #5: Design and order yard signs.

In Charge: Campaign director

When: Ready to distribute two weeks before election day

Resources Needed: Committee members, volunteers, and supporters to order or make and distribute

$:

Activity #6: Children's essay contest

In Charge: Publicity manager

When: Contest runs for ten days early in campaign

Resources Needed: Copy machine and paper, prizes, impartial judges. (Broadcast winning essays on radio as ads.) Obtain cooperation of radio/TV station managers and newspaper editor.

$:

Activity #7: Signature posters

In Charge: Campaign director/chief ambassador

When: Begin circulating them one month before election.

Resources Needed: Each ambassador takes a poster to focus group meetings. All supporters sign them. Compile and deliver to newspaper before election.

$:

Activity #8: Campaign advertising

In Charge: Publicity manager

When: Last two weeks before election

Resources Needed: Cooperation of radio/TV managers, newspapers

$:

Activity #9: Round table or panel discussion on radio/TV/cable
In Charge: Publicity manager
When: Schedule several the last week to ten days before election.
Resources Needed: Committee members, school board members, school
  superintendent, prominent local supporters
$:

Activity #10: Endorsements
In Charge: Campaign director and publicity manager
When: Identify throughout school bond effort. Produce and schedule for
  airing by the week before election day.
Resources Needed: All members and supporters
$:

Activity #11: Letters to the editor
In Charge: Publicity manager
When: Throughout campaign phase
Resources Needed: Interested committee members and supporters write
  letters and have committee critique and coordinate them to prevent re-
  dundancy and fill gaps. Ghostwrite, if necessary.
$:

Activity #12: Campaign letter
In Charge: Publicity manager
When: Last day or so before election
Resources Needed: Input from committee members, distribution by can-
  vassers and other volunteers. Run as ad in newspaper.
$:

Activity #13: Statement from the school board
In Charge: Publicity manager
When: Last day or so before election
Resources Needed: Work with school board members or ghostwrite it for
  their signatures.
$:

Activity #14: March/Rally
In Charge: Campaign director and publicity manager
When: Within last ten days before election
Resources Needed: Ribbon, balloons, signs, float, plenty of supporters
$:

Activity #15: Campaign posters
In Charge: Campaign director
When: Completed and posted within last ten days before election day
Resources Needed: All committee members and volunteers
$:

ACTION PLANNING WORKSHEET

Objective: Canvass

Activity #1: Design and print canvass cards.
In Charge: Canvass coordinator and publicity manager
When: Specific date
Resources Needed: Paper, copy machine
$:

Activity #2: Canvass meeting and rehearsal
In Charge: Canvass coordinator
When: No later than two weeks before election
Resources Needed: Canvass cards, instruction sheets, brochures
$:

Activity #3: Conduct canvass.
In Charge: Canvass coordinator
When: Within two weeks of election
Resources Needed: Volunteers and committee members
$:

Activity #4: Compile and analyze canvass data.
In Charge: Canvass coordinator and secretary-treasurer
When: Specific date
Resources Needed: All committee members. Add identified supporters to
   master list.
$:

ACTION PLANNING WORKSHEET

Objective: Election Day

Activity #1: Phone bank
In Charge: Campaign director
When: All day election day, up to two hours before polls close
Resources Needed: Access to many phones and many volunteers
$:

Activity #2: Poll watching
In Charge: Campaign director
When: While polls are open
Resources Needed: Enough volunteers to watch each precinct
$:

Activity #3: Baby-sitting service
In Charge: Campaign director
When: While polls are open
Resources Needed: Volunteers' homes or a service at each voting location
$:

Activity #4: Rides to polls
In Charge: Campaign director
When: While polls are open
Resources Needed: Volunteers with vehicles
$:

Activity #5: Radio open-mike monitor
In Charge: Publicity manager
When: From week before through election day during live radio programs
Resources Needed: Briefing book and articulate and informed committee
    member
$:

Activity #6: Post-election party (win, lose, or draw)
In Charge: All committee members, volunteers, school board members,
    administrators, supporters
When: After polls close
Resources Needed: Pot luck, refreshments, games
$:

ACTION PLANNING WORKSHEET

Objective: Post-Election Activities

Activity #1: Remove all campaign posters, literature, and litter.
In Charge: Publicity manager
When: ASAP
Resources Needed: Committee members and volunteers
$:

Activity #2: Publicly thank all supporters.
In Charge: Publicity manager
When: ASAP
Resources Needed: Newspaper, radio, TV, and cards
$:

Activity #3: Pay all outstanding debts.
In Charge: Secretary-treasurer
When: ASAP

Resources Needed: Bank statements and bills
$:

Activity #4: File campaign finance reports.
In Charge: Secretary-treasurer
When: ASAP
Resources Needed: Financial records and legal advice
$:

Activity #5: Analyze all available voter data.
In Charge: All committee members
When: ASAP
Resources Needed: Election results by precinct and post-election straw
   poll
$:

Activity #6: Compile scrapbook.
In Charge: Secretary-treasurer and publicity manager
When: ASAP
Resources Needed: Campaign literature, columns, ads, essays, lists of sup-
   porters, volunteers, financial accounts, video, focus group logs,
   newsletters, etc. Write narrative and list opponents and their arguments.
$:

Activity #7: Prepare final report for school board.
In Charge: Publicity manager
When: ASAP
Resources Needed: Recommendations, thank you
$:

A word of warning: when people get wind of a "school improvement committee," some may ask you to address other pressing issues concerning the
school(s). It might be a problem teacher, a dispute over curriculum, or funding a sporting event.

These side issues can bleed you white and scatter your energy. The opposition may even raise these issues as a tactic to distract or confuse the
committee.

Use the action planning worksheets to keep you focused on your specific
goal. Make sure every item placed on the worksheets is directly related to
your primary purpose. To all other issues raised, simply say, "That issue is
beyond the scope of this committee's work. Let's get this new school built
(improved) first before we take on other issues." If appropriate, refer the
problem to the proper authority (such as the school board or principal) for
action.

If the committee's focus becomes diffused, you lose.

Concentrate your energies and work hard. Launch out in new experiments. Never be afraid to have the courage of your opinions. Fix the lines you want to travel along and keep on them.

A. C. Harmsworth, English politician, 1865–1922

3

Surveying the Community

The committee was formed on the belief that school improvement is badly needed. But for the committee's efforts to have some credibility with the people and the school board, you must obtain some sort of mandate.

How strongly does the community feel about the school situation? What does the voter/taxpayer think? (Heaven help you if you try to do his thinking for him!) Are citizens even aware of the desperate condition of the school?

How do you find out what's on their minds? The simplest, most effective way is to conduct a survey.

Surveying the community on school needs and issues is a lot like turning over a rock. All sorts of nasty problems can come to light concerning school facilities and programs. A survey uncovers complaints, misconceptions, old grudges, and unfinished business involving teachers, school administrators, parents, students, the school board, and previous school bond campaigns.

There is also treasure under the rock in the form of constructive criticism, honest opinions, suggestions, and questions for which you will need to find accurate answers. It is even important to discover how many people are completely unaware of any problems in the old school.

WHY A SURVEY?

There are four good reasons to conduct a survey.

First, the survey introduces the committee to the public and opens a conversation on school improvement. The community becomes engaged in the debate from the beginning. This gives people a feeling of ownership in the project. It makes all community members feel included and that their opinions are important. "We're all in this together."

Second, a survey gives the committee a good sense of what the people think about school issues. It gauges the public's awareness of school problems. It measures the strength of support for school improvement. It gathers suggestions for how school problems can be solved.

Third, a survey is a golden opportunity to find supporters and volunteers not rounded up in your initial talent search. Those who express strong support on the survey can be invited to join the effort.

Finally, a survey might be just the right tool to galvanize the community or light a fire under a reluctant school board.

WHAT KIND OF SURVEY IS RIGHT FOR YOU?

If you have tons of time, energy, and volunteers, you can conduct the survey door to door. You are guaranteed a large response, but people may not tell you to your face what is really on their minds. You need to visit a thorough sampling of all areas of the city so survey results are not skewed by neighborhood, race, or economic status.

If you have more money than time, you can mail out the survey and tally the returns. But don't count on a great response or accurate results. Response to mail-in questionnaires is usually small. People who do return them often are those who have strong feelings, pro or con. Those who are content, ignorant, or apathetic about the survey subject tend not to respond.

The most efficient and accurate survey method is by telephone. Nearly everyone has at least one, and, unless you cannot connect, nearly everyone has some opinion. If a person answers that he neither knows nor cares about the school, that in itself is a valid response.

Many people will voice opinions on the phone they would never say in person. These opinions likely will be the ones they carry into the voting booth.

Check with the school superintendent to see whether money might be available to fund a professional survey. If you are lucky, the school board, teacher's union, local economic development foundation, or a service organization can be persuaded to fund the survey. But count on the committee members doing it.

Public funds can be used for the survey if it is conducted to gather information only. They cannot be used to campaign for a school bond. If tax money is to be used, carefully check the survey to ensure none of the

questions are leading or persuasive. Don't provide opponents with the argu-
ment that taxpayers' dollars were used for campaign purposes.

HOW TO PUT TOGETHER A SURVEY

The survey should be short, taking no longer than three minutes to complete.
If it is too short, you will not collect adequate information. If it is too long,
respondents will become irritated or bored. Remember, although each call is
short, together they add up to a very time-consuming task.

A well-designed survey will yield a treasure trove of valuable information.
A poorly worded one can lead to nothing but trouble. The committee must
decide exactly what it needs to know and then carefully craft questions to
gain that information. Beware of questions that are vague or open to more
than one interpretation. Unclear questions lead to confusing answers. If opponents can find a way to distort the survey results, they will use the results
against you.

The purpose of the survey is to gather information. Survey questions must
not lead the respondent in any way. This is not the time to persuade anyone
to change his opinion or take any particular course of action.

Leave space at the end of the survey for personal responses and suggestions. These comments will be included in the survey report you will make
to the school board.

Remember, you may have only this chance to discover what the public has
on its collective mind. Unless you have enormous energy and a huge volunteer staff, you will not survey again.

To get you thinking, a sample phone survey is shown in Figure 3.1. It also
can be used to survey those who attend focus group meetings. Customize
your survey to fit your community's situation or needs.

If the respondent takes the time to make special comments, write them down.
Repeat them back to ensure you have collected them accurately and to let the
respondent know you were listening and getting the information right.

WHO SHOULD YOU CALL?

The survey form is complete and ready to go. How do you decide who will
be surveyed? Again, if you have tons of volunteers and a small school district, you can divide up the phone book listings for everyone in the district.
Unfortunately, it is often not that simple.

School Improvement Survey

Hello, I'm (*name*) calling for (*committee name*). We are polling school district (*name/#*) residents to find out your views on our local public school(s). Everyone's opinion is important. Would you please take part in a three-minute survey? (If not now, is there a more convenient time to call you?)

1. Are you a registered voter? Yes/No
2. What is your age (list age groups)?
3. Are you a homeowner? Yes/No
4. Do you have children attending schools? Yes/No
5. Do you have grandchildren attending schools? Yes/No
6. Do you think improvement is needed in the school facilities at (name) school(s)? Yes/No
7. What do you think of the overall condition of the school building(s) (circle one):
   Excellent   Good   Fair   Poor   Unsure/Don't know
   Comment:
8. How would you rate the condition of the school(s) facilities?
   5. Excellent   4. Good   3. Fair   2. Poor   1. Unsure/Don't know
   a. Handicapped access
   b. Health and safety
   c. Cost of maintaining the building(s)
   d. Classroom size
   e. Adequate overall space (cafeteria, hallways)
   f. Playground/athletic fields size
   g. Comfort of students
   h. Safety of student pickup/dropoff area
   i. Can you think of other problems related to the school facilities?
9. What improvements would be important to you in the school facilities?
10. Is the location of the school important to you? Yes/No
    If a new site is chosen to build a new school, which of the following locations would you prefer? (List options alphabetically to avoid weighing choices.)
    1. (Option)
    2. (Option)
    3. (Option)
    Other   No preference
11. If enough support is found to launch a school bond initiative, would you be willing to support it? Yes/No/Unsure/Depends On
12. (If yes to 11) If a school bond is proposed, would you be willing to volunteer some time to help it succeed? Yes/No
13. Would anyone else in your household like to take a separate survey? Yes/No
    (Spouse concurs)

continued

continued

Name: Phone:
Address:
                    Thank You Very Much For Your Time
(Additional comments):
Other pertinent questions might be:

How long has it been since you were inside the school?
On a scale of 1 to 10, 10 being the best, how do you rate the performance of the school
    district in the following areas:
    Efficient use of funds
    Responsiveness to suggestions and criticism
Sex: Male   Female

Figure 3.1   School Improvement Survey

Districts are often fragmented and don't correspond with phone listings. Usually property taxes are the primary means of support for schools, but some property owners do not reside or vote in the district. For more complete information, you can collate local telephone listings with school district landowner lists. But this gets complicated and very time-consuming.

The simplest way to survey is to call only registered voters within the school district. After all, these are the people who are directly affected—and taxed—for school improvement. They are the ones who are eligible to vote in a school bond election.

Ask the county clerk for a current alphabetized list of all registered voters in the school district. This is public information available free or for a small fee.

Hang on to the original registered voter list! This will serve as your master list. On it you will post the names of all supporters and volunteers identified during the survey, focus group meetings, and campaign activities.

In smaller towns, or if you have many volunteers, try to contact all the registered voters. In larger cities and towns, call only a random sample—say, a certain portion of each letter of the alphabet.

Divide a copy of the list evenly among committee members. Each in turn will make the calls or divide up his portion among volunteers.

If the task proves too much for you, or if you run into difficulty with time or other commitments, ask spouses and friends to help. If you cannot finish making your calls before the deadline, don't hesitate to tell the survey coordinator.

On the other hand, if you find you like surveying, or if you have extra time or helpers, let the survey coordinator know.

But no fair shirking!

Set a tight time limit of ten days to two weeks to conduct the survey. Why? For most of us, the prospect of phoning strangers to ask thorny questions will seem about as much fun as a visit to the dentist. The sooner it's over, the better.

Also, if the survey drags on, touchy people or known opponents will suspect their opinions are being avoided.

The week before it is to begin, heavily advertise the survey. Write news releases or ask newspaper reporters to write a story. Ask local radio or television stations to broadcast public service announcements (see chapter 5, Publicity).

Make sure the public is aware that the survey results will be presented to the school board and made public.

MAKING THOSE CALLS . . .

The survey will be the committee's first direct contact with the community at large. It is vital to make a good first impression.

Surveyors should rehearse the questionnaire before beginning to make the calls. Callers must have pleasant voices, even tempers, and plenty of patience.

Surveyors must never campaign or express personal opinions. You are seeking opinions, not trying to sway them. *At this stage, the committee officially has no opinion.*

Neither must surveyors allow themselves to be drawn into arguments with respondents. Debating serves no purpose, wastes time, and can lead to hard feelings.

Faithfully follow the script of the survey. Go through the questions in a business-like, friendly manner. If a respondent becomes abusive or overly rude, simply thank him for his time and hang up.

Be sure to write down the names and numbers of those who express support for school improvement and those who are willing to volunteer.

Try hard to contact all the people on your list. The best time to catch people at home is Sunday afternoon. If there is no answer, call back at least twice at different times. Avoid calling at normal mealtimes or during big televised sporting events. Never call too late in the evening or too early on weekend mornings.

Although you will never reach everyone, give it your best effort. Don't give up at the first busy signal or no pickup. Mark those numbers and move on to the next. Try them again later.

If you ring up an answering machine, leave a message inviting the resident to call you back to fill out a survey. Leave your name and phone number. Try that number again later.

WHAT TO DO WITH THE RESULTS

Each pollster should tally the results of his calls. You can use a blank survey form. The survey coordinator will combine all tally sheets. He will gather the names of all the volunteers and supporters gleaned from the survey and give them to the secretary-treasurer for his master list.

Do not release partial results before the survey is complete. This could distort the outcome and anger those who have yet to be contacted.

The committee will report the survey results to the school board at its next scheduled meeting. If that is too far off, deliver your finished report to the superintendent. In a cover letter, explain the survey and explain the results.

As an attachment to the report, include all comments, opinions, and remarks of those surveyed.

The survey results will be released to the community through the media the following day.

SURVEY SHORTCOMINGS

Surveys can be dangerous. You are asking people to express opinions without much forewarning or forethought. The results may show strong preferences for options that are clearly not in the long-term best interest of the school or the community.

Those surveyed who are poorly informed of problems facing the school may resist change. For example, many respondents may nostalgically prefer to have the old schoolhouse fixed up, even though cost and usable space would make a new school building a much more sensible alternative.

Others will oppose an increase in taxes for any reason. Those without children in public school may feel no obligation to fund school improvements.

Is the committee obligated to support the majority opinion, even if it is not in the community's best interest? If the committee goes against the will of the majority, is there any chance for bond passage? Can resistance be overcome enough during the education and campaign phases to win on election day?

The school board would be wise to take the survey results seriously. The board should carefully assess the public's comments and suggestions. It should pay close attention to the people's priorities for school improvement. If the district places its priorities, however great and logical, ahead of the electorate's "perceived" greatest needs, it is headed for trouble. Neither should the committee or school board be scared off by a small but noisy opposition. These naysayers likely are not speaking for the majority of citizens.

WATERSHED

With the survey results in hand, the committee has reached a major turning point. Does public sentiment favor change/improvement? Is support strong enough for the committee to continue its efforts? Can school problems exposed by the survey be corrected without a bond issue? Is it time to disband the committee and wait for a more auspicious alignment of the planets?

Don't be fooled by a strong response in favor of a school bond. Some early support will fall away over side issues, such as new school site, conflict with a school board member, rising regional unemployment, or "sticker shock." It's easy for people to say they want improvement in the schools, but getting the majority to vote for a specific plan with a big price tag is another matter.

The most common arguments against school improvement are that it will cost too much or that the district wastes too much money already. These are not good enough reasons to call it quits.

If the school board is ambivalent or resistant, even in light of a strong mandate, this can be a major problem. It is very difficult to pass a school bond over the strong objections of even one school board member.

You might have to wait until after the next school board election, before which you work hard to elect supporters of school improvement.

Now is the time to decide whether to continue your quest or to disband.

If you disband, put together a final report for the school board. Compile a scrapbook of the committee's efforts so far, including committee members, survey results, research, a list of potential supporters and volunteers, and so on.

You've put in a fair amount of effort already. You don't want to have to repeat it next time. The school problems will not go away. There will be a next time . . .

Still there? Then it is time to begin phase II, the education phase.

The survey results will come in very handy in helping you build the education phase strategy.

If the survey shows people to be unaware of school problems, the committee will plan school open-house tours and emphasize problems in the audiovisual presentation (see chapter 6, Audiovisual Presentation).

If the location of the school is a major problem, the committee will work hard to resolve it by exploring the pros and cons of various sites (see chapter 8, Special Interests, Special Issues).

If the community includes a large bloc of elderly residents, private schools, or a large ethnic minority, the committee will work to address the specific concerns of each group.

It's time to peer into the past and begin to dig for buried treasure.

4

Research

Think of your quest for a winning school bond as a search for buried treasure. A successful election is the prize, but you have to dig deep to reach it.

An important part of the hunt is research. It consists of two distinct types: delving into past history and digging for supporters.

HISTORY LESSONS

According to American philosopher and poet, George Santayana, "Those who cannot remember the past are condemned to repeat it." This couldn't be more true than for the history of school bond campaigns. A missed history lesson could lead to a missed opportunity. You can't afford to pass up a single opportunity to succeed on election day.

Studying previous school bond campaigns will help you to focus on where to dig for maximum treasure and how to avoid barren or dangerous ground. You can save a lot of time, trouble, and heartache by studying what has happened during previous attempts.

Begin your research with a visit to the archives of your local newspaper. Read everything available on each past school bond attempt.

What position did the editor take? Why?

What was the news of the day? What was the state of the economy then, and how does it compare with what is happening now? Has the local situation changed since then? Is the need for school improvement greater? Less? Different?

Study the letters to the editor. What were the citizens' arguments and complaints—pro and con? What was the tone of the letters? Did bickering and ill will mar the debate? Did it affect the outcome of the election? Have controversies and obstacles to passage been resolved? Have major supporters/opponents changed sides or gone away?

Has the district reorganized recently? Are there new members on the school board? Has the board's stance changed on school improvement?

Examine the campaign ads in the paper. Which were effective, provocative, or negative?

Collect the following information for each previous school bond election:

1. Track record
2. Date of election
3. Project design and location
4. Amount of bond
5. Voting results (broken down if possible by precinct or ward)
   a. What side issues muddied the campaign?
   b. Were controversies resolved?
   c. Who were the leaders of past efforts?
   d. Who were the strongest supporters?
   e. What groups or individuals were most opposed?
   f. What were the opposing arguments and complaints?
   g. What was the state of the local, regional, and state economy?
   h. How was the campaign conducted?
   i. Can mistakes be identified?
   j. What campaign strategies worked well? Why?

Next, track down every person you can find who was involved in previous bond efforts, both won and lost. Chances are these leaders will not be on the current committee. Working for school bond passage is a grueling task, and few have the stomach for a second round.

Interview these battered veterans. Were they organized? How? What campaign techniques were effective? Which were a waste of time? Which backfired?

Collect the names of prominent citizens who actively supported past school bond attempts. How did they show their support?

Who were the strong and vocal opponents? How active and organized was the opposition? What did they do to defeat the bond? Has anything happened since to change their minds?

If a scrapbook was compiled for a previous school bond effort, hurray! (See chapter 14, After the Election.) Borrow it and study it thoroughly. If no scrapbook is available, try to collect copies of any campaign literature left over from previous efforts.

Expand your research to neighboring towns. Has a nearby city or town recently held a school bond election? Call the district superintendent and ask for advice. Call those who headed the school bond effort. What strategies, fund raisers, and campaign strategies worked well for them? If they could do it again, what would they do differently? Do they have any advice, suggestions, or warnings?

Are friends or family members aware of school bond campaigns in progress in another state? Subscribe to the newspaper there and track their progress.

Carefully study the unsuccessful school bond initiatives. Can you figure out what went wrong? How might you strengthen your effort? How can you learn from their mistakes?

Steal shamelessly from other communities' successful campaigns. They won't mind! There is much you can learn from others' fits of genius and disastrous errors.

Research will help shape the direction your task. Seek out the voices and events from the past. They can provide valuable help for your future.

DIGGING FOR TREASURE—THOSE "YES" VOTES

The other buried treasure is the "yes" votes. This treasure is what the committee's work is all about. No matter how hard you work and how great the need for school improvement, if you do not identify supporters and get them to cast their votes at the polls, all of your effort will be wasted.

The search for "yes" votes begins when you start your committee work and continues until the polls officially close on election day.

THE 25/50/25 RATIO

An Arab proverb goes, "All mankind is divided into three classes: those that are immovable, those that are moveable, and those that move." Today we call this the 25/50/25 rule. For nearly every subject under the sun, this rule holds true.

About 25 percent of any group will oppose any given issue placed before them. These "immovables" will come up with 500 reasons to oppose school improvement. You may knock down one reason, but members of this group will quickly raise another.

To try to change the minds of the negative 25 percent is largely a waste of time. Worse, you may arouse them to organize their own campaign or at least to go to the polls to vote "no." Try not to antagonize or motivate them (see chapter 9, Opposing Views).

Another 25 percent of the citizens will be in favor of school improvement. Unless the proposal is outrageously out of line, the "movers" will support it. Don't take this group for granted and assume they will find their way to the polls on their own. Your task with this group will be to make sure they actually "move" to the polls on election day.

Unless your community's economic, political, or social situation has changed greatly since the last election, the positive and negative blocks will stay largely unchanged.

The remaining 50 percent could vote either way or not at all.

During the education and campaign phases, the committee's effort must concentrate on these "movables." It is crucial to your success. Your job is to inform and motivate them to vote in favor of the school bond referendum.

Consider each potential "yes" vote as a gold doubloon. Some will be easy to find—the strong, active supporters. Others will not be too hard to find—uninformed supporters. Still others are buried deep—apathetic or undecided voters. Your mission is to find them, wake them up, and make sure their votes make it into the ballot box.

WHERE TO DIG FOR SUPPORT

Studies have shown that those most inclined to vote in a school bond referendum are:

- Voters with school-age children living at home
- Citizens interested in school affairs
- Homeowners with mortgages
- Younger to middle-aged citizens (21 to 45 years old)
- Married
- White-collar employed
- People with some higher education
- People with average or higher income
- People active in their community (organizations, church)

Of these voters, the following are most likely to favor school improvement:

- Parents with children attending the school(s) in question
- Moderate, liberal, and independent voters
- Professionals, clerical workers, and homemakers
- Those with positive attitudes toward the school's teaching staff, administration, program efficiency and effectiveness, and operations
- Long-term residents firmly rooted in the community
- Those more politically active and attentive

These are the people you must concentrate on. The more information you can gather about your potential supporters, the more closely you can target your campaign.

Where do you find them?

No one votes in a vacuum. Each voter is influenced by the news he hears, the people he lives and works with, and the groups in which he participates. People are swayed by "significant others" such as spouses, parents, friends, teachers, employers, clergy, and fellow club members.

Try to identify groups, clubs, or congregations where potential supporters get together. These are the groups the committee will make a special effort to contact. Study the focus group reports brought in by the committee's ambassadors. Which groups most strongly favor school improvement? (See chapter 7, Ambassadors Club.)

What neighborhoods hold concentrations of supporters? Visit the county clerk or whoever keeps voting records for your district. Examine the results of previous bond elections. Which wards or precincts voted most heavily? Which areas most strongly favored past bond issues?

Visit your local library or surf the Internet. Check out the most recent census. What are the characteristics of the voters? Organizations? Institutions? Businesses? What is their sex, age, neighborhood, lifestyle, and income level? What organizations do they belong to?

Visit your local chamber of commerce. Is there available a demographic model of your area?

On a map of your community, plot those areas with large support and high voter turnout. Mark pockets of supporters in areas with lower voter turnout. These are the geographic areas that will need special attention.

You already have the list of voters registered in the school district that you used during the phone survey (see chapter 3, Surveying the Community). This will be your master list for the coming campaign.

The secretary-treasurer will maintain the list, adding names of supporters as they become known. This is a "living" document, changing and growing throughout the school bond effort.

As you encounter supporters who are not registered to vote, add their names to the bottom of the master list. During the campaign phase you will offer them a golden opportunity to register.

OTHER PLACES TO DIG FOR TREASURE

High school students will generally favor school improvement. Taxes are not yet an issue for them, and they are very much aware of the bats in the gym and the clanking pipes in their classrooms.

Many high school seniors are eligible to vote, but few will be registered. For many, the school bond election will be their first voting opportunity. Make the most of this.

Contact the high school principal. Ask if your ambassadors might give short civics lessons to the American government, history, or social studies classes on each citizen's privilege and duty to vote. Pass out instruction sheets on how, where, and when to register.

If the principal demurs, ask him to contact the civics, history, and social studies teachers and ask them to give a lecture on a citizen's responsibility to vote. Suggest a field trip to the registrar's office. This makes an excellent lesson in good citizenship.

When encouraging high school students to register, be careful not to ask for their support for the school bond. Get them registered during the education phase and worry about their votes later.

Many *college students* will support your cause. They are not yet homeowners or serious taxpayers. Their memories are fresh of the shortcomings of their old alma mater.

How do you track them down?

Start early. This is a time-consuming project, but it can pay off handsomely in "yes" votes.

Set volunteers the task of studying high school yearbooks from the past three years or so for each school in the district. Use your extensive volunteer network to locate recent high school graduates who are attending college locally and are still living with their parents. Contact those students and encourage them to register to vote.

Most students who are away at college still claim their parents' home as their permanent residence. Most will not be registered to vote, nor would they take an active interest in the school bond on their own.

Call the parents to find out where those students are. Collect their college addresses or ask the parents to forward your campaign packet to them.

If a homecoming celebration, class reunion, or a school break occurs before the election, organize a voter registration opportunity for them. See the county registrar to find out how to set up a voter registration booth. Contact the students at home and inform them of this special chance to register.

Shortly before the election, send the students a short, concise letter stating the case for the bond issue (see appendix B). Include complete instructions on how to register and to request an absentee ballot. Enclose a voter registration card and a stamped envelope addressed to the registrar of voters.

Make it as easy as possible for students to register and to request absentee ballots. Otherwise most won't follow through.

Try to time your pitch to student voters to be in advance of registration and/or absentee ballot application deadlines but close enough to election day that you can provide complete information on the bond (cost, election date, design plan). Without an "ACT NOW!" sense of urgency, it's likely your message will get lost in the school rush.

Each state will have a different set of regulations and deadlines, so check with your local registrar well in advance.

Absentee voters are a fertile source of "yes" votes. Of those you can motivate to cast absentee ballots, most will be in favor of the bond issue. They are not likely to be approached long distance by the opposition.

If a supporter tells you he plans to be out of town on election day, encourage him to vote early (if your state allows this) or with an absentee ballot. Remember, every single vote counts. You must not consciously allow a single "yes" vote to escape uncast.

Local *business people* carry considerable weight in every community. Their active support is very important to school bond success.

Work hard to identify supporters in the business sector. Visit with them at their places of business, at chamber of commerce meetings, and where they meet for other community action and service organizations (Women's Club, Lions, Rotary, Jaycees, etc.). You will have jobs for them during the campaign, such as endorsements and distributing campaign information (see chapter 11, The Campaign).

Treasure hunting should begin early in the committee's work. The more history you unearth, the more closely you can target your campaign. The more you research past voting habits, the easier it will be to gather those "yes" votes in your treasure chest—the ballot box.

Don't consciously pass by or let a single potential "yes" vote slip away. It may be the very one that puts the school bond over the top.

> *There is a way to look at the past. Don't hide from it. It will not catch you if you don't repeat it.*
>
> Pearl Bailey, American singer, 1918–1990

5

Publicity

While the word is yet unspoken, you are master of it; when once it is spoken, it is master of you.

Arab Proverb

Never underestimate the apathy of the American electorate. It may be hard to believe, but while you are throwing your heart and soul into this school project, most people won't show the slightest interest. Of the ones who are interested, some will look for reasons to reject it. Others will be attracted to misinformation, outrageous rumors, or fantastic exaggerations. Still others will make up their minds early and then refuse to listen to further debate. Strong words, but sadly they are true.

Don't despair. The vast majority of Americans are reasonable people of good will. If they are made aware of a great problem and come to realize the problem is their own, they will vote outside their narrow self-interest to solve it.

It is publicity's job to catch people's attention, awaken their interest, provide them with ample reason to support school improvement and, finally, urge them to go to the polls and vote "yes."

Through publicity the committee produces columns, articles, editorials, and news releases in the local newspapers; public service announcements on radio, television, and cable bulletin boards; and perhaps a newsletter and a web page.

Publicity lines up endorsements and writes text for handouts, posters and signs, a video or slide presentation, focus group materials, and campaign literature.

Publicity promotes committee-sponsored community activities, meetings, and events.

THE PUBLICITY MANAGER

The publicity manager wears many hats, but all of them deal with communication. His job consists of placing the committee's name and message before the public and keeping it there. He dreams up every imaginable way to spread the word to as many voters as he can as often as possible.

Through various media he helps educate the community of the need for school improvement. As project options and choices become available, he explains them to the public. He keeps everyone informed of the latest developments and promotes committee activities and events.

The publicity manager must be articulate, tactful, honest, and even tempered. This is hardly the position for the hothead, the temperamental artist, or the poison pen!

The publicity manager should have some knowledge of public relations, but don't let this scare you. Media experience is very helpful, but it is not necessary.

He must have one essential asset—stamina. Publicity is a continuous, time-consuming effort from day one through election day. He must be prepared for the long haul.

The publicity manager coordinates all publicity for the committee, but he should not be expected to do it all alone. Every week someone must produce a heap of sparkling, pithy prose. All committee members, supporters, and even opponents (indirectly, for the sake of argument) should be tapped for bright ideas. Anyone who comes up with a topic for the column or newsletter should be encouraged to pursue it. The publicity manager is going to need all the help he can get!

To avoid crossed signals and duplicate effort, all media contacts should be cleared through the publicity manager. But again, he should not stand alone. Although it will not always be possible, he must try hard to run all written or audiovisual material by the committee for critique and approval before it goes public. This may seem like a nuisance, but catching errors and mixed messages before they become public can save many headaches later.

If you discover a mistake after it has gone out in the world, correct it as quickly as possible. The community's trust in you is critical to your success. It's better to correct your own errors than to let the opposition point them out for you.

Likewise, as false rumors and misinformation surface, respond to them at once with the facts. This is where research into past campaigns comes in handy (see chapter 4, Research). Who were the leading opponents and what were their arguments? How did they make their appeal to voters? Doing research prepares the publicity manager to anticipate and swiftly counter opposition with truth and light.

WHAT'S IN A NAME?

Beginning with the education phase, the committee should adopt a formal name, slogan, logo, and color. The purpose is to produce instant and easy recognition. They should be designed to stand out from the myriad events and issues vying for people's attention every waking minute. The committee's name can be catchy—KIDS for Keep Improving District Schools or SOS for Save Our Schools—or straightforward—Yourtown School Needs Committee.

The logo should be simple, attractive, upbeat, and clearly related to your project.

The slogan should be lively and, again, directly related to your project: "Blue Ribbon Schools for Blue Ribbon Kids" or "Lets 'Bond' Together For Our Future" or "The Name is Bond, School Bond. Give this district the license to build." You get the idea.

Whatever you decide on for name, logo, and slogan, focus on the kids.

The committee's official color might be the school colors or patriotic colors. It must be distinctive, positive, and not confused with other campaigns or movements. Choose a color that the public will come to instantly associate with the committee.

The committee name, slogan, logo, and color will appear wherever possible in all media: stationery letterhead, newsletter, newspaper column, web site, buttons, campaign ribbons, posters, yard signs, pencils, bumper stickers, and billboards.

To design these items, it helps to have a committee member or volunteer who has experience in graphic design and/or computer graphics. This saves time and money. Graphics give your message more of a kick and make it quicker to recognize and easier to remember.

Your Message

The community needs a new (renovated, enlarged) school. Why? How big or extensive? How much will it cost? Where will it be located?

At first there will be no definite design or plan. This will only become clear after seeking community consensus and meeting with the teachers, the staff, and the school board.

Publicity will follow the three-phase format of the project:

- *Information phase:* Begin by introducing the committee to the public. Explain how you plan to gather information and citizens' opinions on the possible need for a new school (renovation, addition). Keep the public informed of your progress.
- *Education phase:* Discuss facts about the current school situation. Report on the decisions made toward school improvement—designs, sites, costs.
- *Campaign phase:* Sell the school bond proposal to the voters. Explain to each voting bloc the reasons why the community needs a new (improved) school.

Relate every aspect of each phase to the kids. Are the children losing opportunities for a modern education because of outdated facilities? Are students studying in hazardous or very unpleasant conditions (overcrowding or bats in the library)? Are the best teachers looking elsewhere for jobs in better school facilities? Is the current school discouraging quality job applicants for local business?

Publicity will focus on how school improvement will benefit the entire community. What is the role of good schools in attracting business and quality candidates for local jobs? Are other communities getting ahead at your town's expense because of poor school facilities? Is the community losing businesses and top-notch professionals who are discouraged by the school situation? What are the long-term consequences of doing nothing about the old school(s)?

Taking Your Message to the People

How do people in your city or town get their news? Unless citizens are hermits living in caves, they receive information daily from one or more of the following sources. Here are the advantages, disadvantages, and ways for publicity to use each:

- *Television:* The most popular news source is television. It provides instant exposure through pictures and sound. Commercial TV is the most expensive type of advertising. Public service announcements are broadcast free, but there are very limited opportunities to use them.

Panel discussions and interviews are broadcast free. Does your city have a local bulletin board on cable TV? Check with the cable company and the chamber of commerce or city hall for ways to display information there. Does the school district have a cable page? It can be used to educate school employees and the community-at-large about the bond issue. *Note:* It is illegal to use public school–sponsored media for campaign purposes. This source shares information only.

- *Radio:* Radio has a large audience with flexible programming. You can customize your message for specific listening groups: country, youth (rock/pop), retired (easy listening), religious, ethnic (Spanish language), and so on. It also costs less than television but usually more than the newspaper. Public service announcements, interviews, and panel discussions are broadcast free.
- *Newspaper:* Generally the local circulation is large. A newspaper provides full, detailed information and can be illustrated with photos or artwork. Advertising costs are reasonable. A weekly newspaper column and frequent news articles and news releases will keep the committee's activities continuously in the public eye. They are printed free as news.
- *Computer:* More and more homes have computers and Internet access. Computer users are generally a better-informed audience that is more likely to vote and support school improvement. A committee web site is a place where you can post columns and newsletters, answer questions via e-mail, and list upcoming committee events and activities. Public access to the committee's web site is easy and free. Does the city and/or school district host a web site or electronic bulletin board where you can post news and announcements? (The same restrictions will apply on information posted).
- *Newsletter:* A newsletter contains timely and varied information. It is flexible, with many opportunities for wide distribution. A quality product can be assembled at a very reasonable cost.
- *Direct mail:* This type of mail can be closely focused on the target audience (voters in the affected school district). Mass mailing can be expensive and may be confused with junk mail.
- *Outdoor signage:* Billboards, marquees, bulletin boards, signs, and posters provide inexpensive and good exposure to all citizens.

USING THE MEDIA FOR MAXIMUM EFFECT

There are several ways to use the media to your advantage: a newspaper column, news releases, public service announcements, news coverage of your activities and events, paid advertising, and letters to the editor. The first three are discussed here. Letters and ads are examined more fully in chapter 11, The Campaign.

Newspaper Column

If you can convince the local newspaper to carry a weekly column of your committee's activities, you have greatly smoothed your path to success.

Why a column? It introduces the committee to the community and keeps your efforts in the public eye. Having a space in the same place at regular intervals in the newspaper allows you to deliver a lot of detailed information to the public. People will come to expect it and look to the column for accurate and timely information.

The committee can use the column to anticipate and answer every conceivable question that comes up about the project. It keeps people informed of what the committee is doing and why.

How do you start a column? First, ask for an appointment with the editor of the local newspaper. Introduce yourself and describe the committee, its mission, and its goals. Let him know why you believe the committee's work is newsworthy and important to his readership.

Ask for the editor's support. Request weekly space in the paper for around 600 to 800 words. Be ready to supply him with a list of topics and samples of your writing style.

What will be in the column? Topics will reflect your three-phase approach to the bond: information, education, and campaign (see appendix B for column topic ideas). Special events, contests, and activities can be announced in the column. You can use it to get committee members invited to group meetings to make presentations (see chapter 7, Ambassadors Club).

Every column must contain an invitation to all citizens to attend your meetings. Each column should encourage interested supporters to join the committee or volunteer to help.

Include at least one contact phone number where people can express opinions or make comments and suggestions. It is important to avoid the slightest hint of exclusion or secrecy.

For an extra bonus, pitch the column to the local radio stations. If they agree to read your columns as public service announcements, marvelous! Check with your local cable company about use of the community channel. Perhaps you can get scrolling message space for your column.

News Release

The news release, or NR, is an item you prepare and give to the press (newspaper). It is an effective way to get your message out to the community. If the editor uses it, you've gotten your message out for free. Besides, the reader usually trusts a "news" article more than an advertisement, opinion piece, or letter to the editor.

A disadvantage of the NR is there is no guarantee the editor will use it as written—or use it at all. He is free to rewrite it, use part of it, include it in another article, or throw it away.

The NR has a specific format so the busy editor knows exactly what it is when it arrives on his desk. The title tells the editor the main topic. The first paragraph contains a summary of all the information that will follow: who, what, where, when, why, and how. *Note:* Don't leave anything out. Incomplete news can be worse than none at all. Carefully craft this first paragraph. It is the one that either grabs the editor—and the reader—or lets him get away.

The rest of the copy expands on the first paragraph, working from the most important to the least important information. The editor may have to whack off the end to fit his available space, so don't save the best until last.

The NR must cover one topic only. Ideally its length is no more than one page. If you need more space, include a background or fact sheet (see sample in appendix B).

The NR contains information, not a sales pitch. It is "news" not an advertisement—just the facts, no opinions. But careful wording of the "news" can very effectively promote school improvement.

How do you boost your chances that the media will use your NR?

- The topic must be timely. Old news is no news. Submit the NR well in advance of that committee-sponsored street fair.
- Give the NR a novel angle. For example, if school attendance has reached record levels, this could be your hook for the topic of overcrowding in the school. If the school building is "celebrating" its 75th anniversary, this is the perfect opportunity to slip in a description of its outdated classroom technology.
- Include quotes from experts and opinion leaders in the NR. Quotes from prominent citizens and celebrities attract attention and carry a lot of weight. You can "sneak" opinions into the NR through quotes.

Public Service Announcement

The public service announcement (PSA) is used by radio and television on "community bulletin boards" and as fillers. The PSA can reach a broad audience and can be tailored to reach specific groups. It is generally used to invite the public to a specific event or meeting. Best of all, it is broadcast free as a public service to nonprofit organizations and causes.

The PSA is much shorter than the news release (see appendix B for sample and format). It is timed to be read in 10, 20, 30, or 60 seconds.

The listener, unlike the reader, cannot reread or clip the announcement for future reference, so the PSA must be written differently than a news release. To give a PSA more impact:

- Use clear, simple, short sentences.
- Mention twice the essential information, such as the date and location of the event, the committee's name, and a contact phone number.
- Stick to a single subject and one main point.
- Grab the listener and inspire action. Your lead sentence should be an attention-grabber.
- Use a personal, conversational tone, the way people speak to one another. Speak to the listener as "you."
- Put a bit of passion into it. A little tug on the heartstrings can have a strong effect on the listener.
- Don't be afraid to use humor when appropriate. A PSA is one place where cute and perky can work well as long as it doesn't get in the way of the information.
- Avoid getting too technical or detailed. Listeners will quickly tune out.
- Use short, simple words wherever possible. Remember syllables equal time, and the meter is running.
- Use a positive appeal instead of a negative one. Avoid words such as "never," "no," and "don't."
- Write out words, rather than abbreviate. "St." can confuse the announcer. Does it mean street or saint or first?
- Use punctuation to create pauses, emphasis, and special effects.
- Make every word count.

To attract more attention to the PSA, recruit a prominent local citizen or celebrity, such as the mayor or a popular disc jockey, to read your message on the air. Or ask a student to read the PSA. After all, kids are what the school bond is all about.

If it's all right with the radio or TV station, send a tape recording along with your script or arrange for the reader to record the message at the station.

Try to place the news release or PSA in the proper hands fully two weeks before the subject event. This should give the station ample time to schedule air time.

Double-space the copy on standard-size plain white paper in black ink. Leave ample margins all around. If the committee has letterhead, use it. Avoid gimmicks such as crazy fonts and brightly colored paper or ink. They will annoy the manager/editor.

The final paragraph (NR) or sentence (PSA) should contain details about the committee, its mission, and who to contact for further information. If you must go to a second page (NRs only), type "-MORE-" centered on the bottom of the first page. On the top of the second page, abbreviate the headline and the page number. At the end, type "# # #" or "-END-" or "-30-". For NRs, capitalize and underline the title. For PSAs, capitalize the entire text. Neither news item requires a cover letter. (See appendix B for samples.)

All this said, the format for NRs and PSAs is not carved in stone. Concentrate on providing the editor with clean professional copy. High-quality content is what will command attention and respect.

MEDIA COVERAGE OF ACTIVITIES AND EVENTS

Now that you've invited the public to come to your party, parade, or pie eating contest, you'll want news of it to reach the most people possible. Not only do you want to invite everyone to come, you want the media to show those folks who stayed home what they missed.

Plan ahead. Call the newspaper and radio and TV stations well in advance of important committee events, activities, and photo opportunities. Talk to the assignment editor rather than individual reporters. The assignment editor is the one who decides what events are covered on a given day. Request that a reporter or news crew attend. Make a reminder call on the morning of the event.

If possible, schedule your event at a time that is convenient for the media. Find out the newspaper's deadline to allow ample time for the paper to prepare a news article of your event. If you hope to receive TV coverage, allow plenty of time for film editing before local TV newscasts.

If you expect to receive video coverage for your event, orchestrate the visual image to convey your message in a clear, positive way. A television news broadcast will usually include no more than a few seconds of your event. They will concentrate on the simple and superficial. Thus, if you are to be interviewed as a "talking head," set the stage for maximum impact.

Decide in advance what you want to say. Prepare and rehearse several short, simple, well-crafted statements or "sound bites." Make every word count. Make your background send a message, too, with a banner or placards.

A committee spokesperson should be on hand to supply reporters with whatever information they need for complete and accurate coverage. Provide a detailed, well-written fact sheet to all reporters. This paper should contain facts about the event, background information about the committee and your project, and names and phone numbers of committee contacts who can provide follow-up information.

Background information is particularly welcome to harried, overworked reporters. It saves them time and effort. Besides, background material states your case as you wish the public to hear about it.

TV crews will likely arrive late to your event and will require extra time to set up their equipment. Be flexible. While you wait, lavish attention on the print media. They will require more in-depth information.

Try to locate your event close to television and radio stations or newspaper offices. If that is not possible or you cannot get reporters to come, consider filming the event yourself. Send a videotape to the studio with a typed news release that explains the event.

Remember, around 80 percent of the people get all or most of their daily news from television. If you get TV to cover your events as news, you get powerful coverage of your event—and your project—for free.

Concentrate on making it easy for the media to cover your activities. Taking good care of the news purveyors can pay off in big publicity dividends.

HOW TO DEAL WITH POOR MEDIA SUPPORT

Support for a school bond effort by the local media is crucial. Without local newspaper and radio (and television if available) support, your task will be much more difficult.

What if the newspaper won't cover your activities? What if the editor ignores your news releases? What do you do if the TV or radio station manager won't air your public service announcements or make time for committee interviews or panel discussions?

Don't feel hurt or paranoid if you're turned down. Because the media isn't brimming with enthusiasm doesn't mean they hate you. They may lack space or time or staff. They may have a standing policy forbidding the use of non–staff-written material.

If the media managers balk at outsiders writing for them, or if they say they don't have the space or time, ask for the names of reporters who can serve as liaison.

Not everyone in the media will favor a school bond. Some may oppose it. If they are up-front about it, you must respect that opposition. If the media treats you fairly but without enthusiasm, you have no grounds for complaint. You may even be able to use their negative arguments to more effectively make your case.

But what if an important media outlet refuses to help at all? What do you do if a media outlet totally ignores or deliberately misrepresents your efforts? This can be a serious setback but not an insurmountable one. It makes your job more difficult and time-consuming but not impossible.

Without strong media support, it is extra important for you provide the news outlets with news. It will be much harder for them to ignore your cause if you present them with newsworthy events and activities.

If the committee sponsors a rally, offers an essay contest, or plays a role in some big community celebration, work hard to get the media to cover it and make it difficult for them to slight you. Learn their deadlines and meet them with quality copy. The less editing your writing needs, the more kindly the editor will look upon you. The more exciting and photogenic your events are, the more likely they will be reported and photographed.

Write your own news articles and news releases. Submit photos in the newspaper's stated format. Write your own captions for them. Deliver them in person to the newspaper office well before press time, and place them in the hand of the appropriate bureau chief or editor. Don't leave him wiggle room to misquote committee members or misinterpret your actions.

As often as possible, involve prominent political, business, and community leaders in your activities and events. It is difficult for the editor to ignore a major committee-sponsored event involving the mayor, a state senator, or a popular celebrity. If one news outlet allows another to scoop it, the one left out will think twice before it lets that happen again.

Be polite and a little pushy, but never, never embarrass or insult the media. It is madness to pick a fight with someone who buys ink by the barrel or controls the air waves.

Web Site

Find a volunteer or committee member who knows his way around cyberspace. Ask him to build a simple web site for the committee. A web site enables the committee, through e-mail, to receive and respond to comments, suggestions, complaints, queries, and rumors. On your web site, you can post the newsletters and newspaper columns and announce upcoming events and activities. This is just one more way to communicate with the public.

Make sure the pages load quickly. Online readers are not patient, and they have very short attention spans. Design page graphics and copy to be attractive, simple, and easy on the eye. "Busy"-ness and cuteness can turn off the viewer. Animation is unnecessary and slows down the loading of your pages.

People read on the Internet differently than in the newspaper or newsletter. Copy must be short and direct. Make key points crisply and expand them in one or two sentences. If your webmaster is experienced, he can create links to more in-depth reading such as the newspaper columns, news releases, and newsletters. Make those links simple and logical. Don't forget to include the committee's logo, slogan, and color.

Newsletter

If you have a strong collection of writers on the committee, you might consider producing a series of newsletters. A newsletter is a flexible and efficient way to take your message directly to the public. It is the perfect means to respond quickly to issues as they arise.

Start by collecting newsletters from any and all sources: social and service clubs, businesses, and government agencies. They will help you work out your own format and style. Desktop publishing software nowadays is inexpensive, is simple to use, and can be a great time-saver for newsletter production. But the old cut-and-paste method with graph paper and a paste pot works well enough.

Each newsletter can focus on a single topic, or it can take a potpourri approach. Include at least one news article per issue. Column topics make great newsletter articles.

Use fillers: anecdotes, poems, announcements of upcoming committee activities and events. Short school-related news tidbits from around the country can add more national significance to your efforts. Drawings, clip art, photos, and cartoons are attractive and take up space when the words fall short. Don't forget to include a bit of humor. When used judiciously, humor can improve the delivery of your message.

You might include a "man on the street" comment section. You could quote average citizens and prominent local supporters. Be ever on the lookout for quotes that support your message. For example, "Children are the living messages we send to a time we will not see."

The newsletter can be a great interactive tool between the committee and the public. Include clip-out forms to solicit public comments and suggestions. Print entry forms for contests to invite citizen participation.

Encourage all committee members and supporters to contribute to the newsletter. Their work can be as short as a couple of paragraphs to as long as a full-blown interview of a school board member, a student, or a prominent local supporter (the mayor, chamber of commerce president, etc.). Remember, the more volunteers recruited to write, the more the work will be spread around.

You are limited only by your imagination, time, and budget.

Newsletter Nuts and Bolts

- Prominently display the committee's name, logo, and motto on the masthead of every issue. If you use color, use it sparingly. If you are using a copier, consider printing in black ink on colored paper (the committee's color, of course). No neon colors, please.
- The newsletter must be neat and visually attractive. Left-justified text (flush left, ragged right) is easier on the eye and leaves a bit more white space. Whatever design you choose, it should have a uniform appearance in an easy-to-read typeface or font.
- A two- or three-column format is a nice touch and makes the copy easier to read.
- Avoid writing in the first person—"us," "our," or "we." The newsletter should be written about the committee's activities and mission and not be about the committee.
- Don't be too garish in style or writing. Literary screams and shouts will cause the reader to run away or not take the newsletter seriously. Use italic, bold, and underline styles sparingly.
- Avoid cheap clip art. Scanned or pasted photos and graphs or charts are much better choices.
- Try to publish a consistent number of pages at regular intervals.
- A newsletter can be distributed by hand or by mail. If you plan to mail it, leave space for the address and stamp.

Find places to leave copies of the newsletter where people gather and have time to read. Prime spots are the senior center, public library, city hall lobby, chamber of commerce, supermarket, and discount store bulletin boards. Seek out captive or bored audiences, such as in the laundromat and the doctor's or dentist's waiting room. Always ask the proprietor's permission before posting your literature.

How often newsletters are published depends on the talent and the number of writers and the time available to those preparing it. Publishing twice a month and once a week during the campaign phase would be ideal, but here is a word of caution. Don't bite off more than you can chew. If writing a newsletter will stress out or deplete the energy of the publicity manager and his volunteers, then don't do it. A poorly done newsletter is worse than none at all.

OTHER PUBLICITY DUTIES

The publicity manager is involved in many other tasks, often in conjunction with other subcommittee leaders.

- *The video or audiovisual presentation:* one of your most powerful tools to bring school problems to the people. Unless the committee has the video professionally produced, the publicity manager will coordinate its production (see chapter 6, Audiovisual Presentation). If a video proves to be too large or too expensive a project for the committee, the publicity manager will assemble a slide show or prepare scrapbook materials for focus group presentations.
- *Briefing book:* The publicity manager may or may not personally conduct focus group meetings through the ambassadors club, but he will help to prepare for them. The publicity manager will assemble the written material that goes with the ambassadors to meetings. This packet is a work in progress. It requires constant updating (see chapter 7, Ambassadors Club).
- *Events:* Community events and celebrations are great opportunities for the committee to carry its message to the public, raise money, and have some fun. Publicity will ensure that the public shows up. Activities may include a float in the annual harvest parade, street theater during Summerfest, a booth at the county fair, or a children's essay contest. The entire committee should be involved in dreaming up these events. Use your research to see what was done successfully in the past and what other towns have done. You are limited only by your imagination.
- *Posters:* The publicity manager will design and distribute posters to advertise the events. Display the posters at the usual high-traffic places—supporting businesses, bulletin boards, marquees, billboards). Remove them promptly after each event.

THE CAMPAIGN BROCHURE

The brochure is the single most important piece of literature produced by the committee. It contains vital information the voter will need to make an informed decision. It is the committee's final pitch to the community before the election. Your goal is to place at least one copy in the hand of each eligible voter in the district.

Tips on Brochure Design

Before you begin to build the brochure, collect and study brochures from past local school bond attempts. Call or write school superintendents in surrounding cities, counties, and states that have recently held school bond elections. Ask them to send copies of their brochures.

It doesn't matter if the brochures were used in successful or failed bond attempts. They may not even fit your particular situation. What they do is get your creative juices flowing. They help you decide what your brochure should, and should not, contain. What made the brochures effective? Where did they go wrong? Were they too fancy? Too crude? Too wordy? Incomplete? How might you improve on them?

There are a million details you will want to include in the brochure—everything you believe the voter should know about the proposed bond issue. But remember, people have many other things on their minds besides school improvement. Most will pay precious little attention to the brochure. If the reader is overwhelmed with data, he won't read it at all.

Develop the brochure with the KISS principle in mind: "Keep it slim, simple." The brochure's purpose is to provide the voter with the most important information in the least amount of time (see sample brochure text, appendix D).

Make it reader-friendly with an easy-to-read typeface. You may change print size, but stick with a single font. Cute and fancy can be distracting and irritating. Lay out your text with questions and bulleted answers. This invites the reader to scan them. Topics you should include are:

- What's wrong with the present school?
- How will the proposed bond issue fix the problem?
- Why build now?
- What will it cost?
- What will we get for our money?
- How will school improvement benefit the kids?
- How will school improvement benefit the community?

Be up-front about the money issue, but don't belabor it. Do provide levy rates and valuations, but keep it short. If you include too many financial details, the reader's eyes will glaze over. Avoid the words "cost" and "price" in favor of "investment" and "value."

Present the amount in bite-size terms in simple language. The tax increase on a house worth $XX will be $X. Break it down into yearly, monthly, and daily costs—equivalent to a newspaper subscription or a cup of coffee per day.

People like to see what they are getting for their money. Include the floor plan and the architect's line drawing of the school. These should be available from the school superintendent or architect. If the bond is for expansion or renovation of existing buildings, shade the new and/or improved areas. If it is new, note the new location on a small, simple map.

Include essential voting information: election day date, time, and polling places.

Next, decide how you will distribute the brochure. If you plan to hand deliver only, you can print all over it. But if you plan to mail it, leave blank space for the address, return address, and stamp. Design it to fold in such a way that you won't need an envelope. Stuffing costs more and takes time.

Find a committee member, volunteer, or supporter who is adept at using desktop publishing software. You'll be amazed at what a quality brochure you can produce with these programs. If you provide the printer with a camera-ready product, you will save even more money. If cut and paste is your only option, don't worry. Clean, well-written, reader-friendly copy goes a long way.

Your goal is to place a brochure in the hand of every voter before election day. Depending on your funds and available volunteers, distribute the brochure in any or all the following ways:

- Hand deliver door-to-door during the canvass (see chapter 12, The Canvass)
- Mass mail to all registered voters
- Distribute at the last round of focus group meetings
- Leave stacks of brochures with supportive businesses as handouts to interested clients/customers
- Include as an insert in the "neighborhood shopper" and local newspaper
- Hand out in public places: at shopping centers, on street corners, at special events, at booth at the county fair, to parade spectators

ROLE OF PUBLICITY IN THE CAMPAIGN PHASE

Throughout the education phase, the committee's message has been creeping toward a more persuasive stance. The campaign phase officially begins the day the school board announces a school bond election.

As the committee enters the campaign phase, publicity becomes more important and the publicity manager and helpers must pick up their pace. Not only do the columns and other media contacts continue, but the publicity manager joins the campaign director in producing and distributing campaign materials for the final push.

In the final days before the election, all your plans and preparations come together. It's time to pull out all the stops!

Chapter 11, The Campaign, more thoroughly covers the use of the media during the final weeks before election day. Here are some of the tasks the publicity manager will coordinate:

- *Endorsements:* Now is the time for your community's opinion leaders to come to the aid of the school bond. The publicity manager has solicited and collected the names of prominent supporters since the beginning. It's time to help them prepare their newspaper ads and schedule radio/TV spots for them. Although you will run these ads during the final week to ten days of the campaign, it takes time to organize and prepare them.
- *Campaign letter:* This short letter is signed by all committee members. The committee will buy advertising space for it in the final paper before election day. It is the committee's final pitch to the community to vote "yes" in the bond election. Begin by thanking the community for its support. Make a few telling points in favor of the bond. Urge supporters to vote (see sample in appendix B).
- *Statement from the school board:* It is vital that the community be made aware of the school board's strong support of the bond issue. If they have not already planned to do so, ask the board members to place a letter of support in the final newspaper before election day. Offer to ghostwrite it for the members' signature. Board members must pay for this ad with personal, never district, funds (see sample in appendix B).
- *Paid advertising:* Of course the frequency, length, and size of these ads depend on your budget. The publicity manager will schedule committee-sponsored radio or TV ads as often as possible at regular intervals during the final days before the election. Newspaper ads must appear in the daily newspaper during the final days (or the final edition of the weekly paper) before the election. These include the paid endorsements. The publicity manager will coordinate the size/length, placement, and timing of the ads. Check with the newspaper and radio advertising departments for bulk discounts.
- *Free media events:* This is the time for committee members to conduct panel discussions, sit for interviews, and have the winners of the chil-

dren's essay contest read their essays on the radio or have them printed in the newspaper. With luck you can convince station managers and editors to provide free air time and print space as a public service.

- *Get-out-and-vote poster:* Even strong supporters need a reminder of election day. A poster is very effective if widely distributed right before the election. Design the poster to be bold, simple, and positive. Display it everywhere it is legal (see sample in appendix D).

Be sure to include the committee's name and address on all campaign literature and in all radio, television, and newspaper ads in compliance with state and local election laws. For print media, something like this will do: "Paid for with volunteer contributions by the (Name) Committee, Money Baggs, Treasurer, P. O. Box 123, Yourtown, State, Zip."

For radio spots it is only necessary to mention the committee's and treasurer's names. The treasurer's address must be on file at the radio or television station.

By including "Paid for by private donations" or "Not printed at public expense," you will keep the school district—and the committee—out of trouble.

TIPS FOR POWERFUL COMMUNICATION

Regardless of which methods you use to get your message to the public, keep in mind this general advice:

- Choose a style that is folksy, friendly, and casual—like conversation between neighbors or friends. Your tone should be cheerful and optimistic. It is much easier to agree with someone you like.
- Avoid a tone that is preachy, threatening, or cranky. It will turn people away from your message—and possibly from the school bond.
- Keep your message focused. Your first and foremost concern is the well-being of the school children and the economic growth of the community.
- It is very difficult to overcome self-interest. You must make each citizen aware that the school situation is his problem and that he holds the key to its solution. He must be convinced that it is in his self-interest to support school improvement.
- This may seem contradictory, but your message must be passionate without sounding too emotional. Communicate from the heart, but don't get carried away.

- Never respond in any way to personal attacks. Do not give mean-spirited individuals the satisfaction of a reply.
- When misinformation or ugly rumors come to light, quickly reply with the facts. Respond to statements, not to the people who make them. Remember, you have the high ground. Stay there!
- Use humor whenever appropriate, but never let your wit become mean, sarcastic, or biting.
- Go straight to the point in your very first sentence. Don't beat around the bush. Fifty-word rule: if readers are still reading or listening after 50 words, they will likely stay with it to the end. Those first 50 words must sparkle.
- Put pizzazz in your pitch. People will read long copy or listen to a lengthy speech if it is informative and upbeat.
- Use short, simple sentences of 12 words or less. Vary sentence length and structure.
- Use short, simple words. Avoid trying to impress your audience with your huge vocabulary. Big pompous words will annoy and confuse the reader/listener.
- Spell things out. Coy or cutesy can be a real turn-off.
- If the text is long, break it up. It is easier to read several short sections than one long one. When appropriate, place your information in a bulleted shopping list style or question and answer format. Bullets organize your points and make text easier for the reader to follow.
- In print, choose a font that is easy on the eyes and not too decorative. Use one only to avoid distracting the reader. Different size print is OK, but don't overdo it.
- Underlining, italicizing, and highlighting key words or phrases can be very effective if used sparingly.
- Use color, but don't overdo it. School colors can tie in nicely with your message, and you can't go wrong with the old red, white, and blue. Be careful with red alone. It sets off mental alarms, such as blood, fire, and danger.
- Include eye-catching graphics when appropriate. Make print ads stand out by rounding the corners of the border or having the contents poke through it. Look through newspaper and magazine ads for ideas. What attracts your attention?
- Art work must be easy to understand, simple, and directly related to the school and the students.
- Avoid messy or cluttered text or artwork. Cramming too much together is not reader-friendly. A simple picture or short text with a lot of white space can be very effective.

- A photo is more powerful than a drawing. A photo of children is highly effective.
- Be repetitive. One in every three people who looks at a page of ads will see yours. If you want everyone to see it, run it several times.
- Diversify. Don't do just one thing. Try many different means of catching the community's attention, such as poems, cartoons, jingles, posters, ribbon, balloons.
- Don't make your literature look too slick, especially in very small communities. People might begin to wonder where all the money came from for such a professional look. But it should not be so crude as to distract from the message or to command little attention or no respect.
- Make your pitch a call to action. People are more inclined to act if there is pressure to do something now.

Below are a few of the most persuasive words in advertising. Many will work well for your campaign.

You	Easy
Save	Success
Safety	Simple
Results	Love
Proven	Health
New	Guaranteed
Money or $$	Now

These eye-catching, appealing words change over time. Look through newspapers and magazines and listen to radio and TV ads for the latest batch.

Try to think of the voter as a potential customer. You are "selling" him the school bond. He will "buy" it by dropping his "yes" vote in the ballot box.

If a voter believes he has been ill-served by the committee (lied to, a promise not kept, an important question left unanswered), chances are he will not vote for the bond, and, worse, he will try to talk his friends and relatives out of supporting the school bond as well.

According to a study by the Technical Assistance Research Program (TARP), most customers won't complain, but they will tell an average of 16 people about their bad experience. In your case, that could mean lost support and votes.

The TARP study showed that 97 percent of dissatisfied customers will come back if the problem is solved quickly. They will tell eight people if the problem is solved to their satisfaction, and they will be more loyal than if they had had no problem at all.

Listen to the "customer," the voter. It "costs" five times more effort to find a new supporter than to keep the one you already have. (TARP, 1999)

THE PAPER TRAIL

Publicity will generate mountains of paper: handouts, newsletters, copies of columns, posters, and campaign literature. The cost of copying can add up fast, and it can take a big bite out of tight budgets.

To save on copying costs, check with banks, businesses, or organizations that are friendly to your cause. Ask for free copying privileges.

Rotate around, and try not to hit one business too often. Break up huge print jobs among several copiers. As a courtesy, bring your own paper. Buy it in bulk.

Take extra care that your materials do not end up as litter or in the trash. Please recycle as much as you can.

THE FINAL WORD . . .

. . . is very important! The image you present to the community will be used by citizens to judge not only the committee but also the school bond project. The bond could stand or fall on how the committee relates to the people.

Publicity is the voice that carries the committee's message to the public. Go to great lengths to maintain an honest, positive, and enthusiastic image.

If you don't know the answer to a question concerning the bond issue or the committee's position, don't guess or try to fake it. Tell the inquirer that you don't know but that you'll find out and get back to him. Then follow through.

If the media in general are reluctant to help you, you must focus your efforts on taking your information directly to the people. The personal approach is very effective. You can greatly boost the power of your message through the use of an audiovisual presentation.

6

Audiovisual Presentation

If you can't convince people that there is a compelling need for school improvement, the school bond referendum will not pass.

Most people have a strong urge to hang on to their money. If you are going to convince them to part with it, you must make a forceful case that their money will be well spent on school improvement. How do you convince them to open their wallets? How do you make people aware of the serious shortcomings of the school facilities?

You can, and should, host an open house and conduct tours of the old school(s), but few people will come. Those who do most likely will be supporters.

You can talk until you're blue—and you will—but many people will not listen, or they may fail to grasp the true impact of the school's problems.

During the course of the school bond effort, the committee will assemble a bag of magic tricks. These will include constant publicity, the ambassadors club, special events, and activities. But perhaps the single most important rabbit you can pull out of your hat is an audiovisual (AV) presentation.

An AV presentation brings the school to the people. It takes them on a virtual tour of the school and shows them things they didn't know. It shows and tells. It encourages people to look at a situation they might rather not face. It will be the centerpiece of the ambassadors' focus group meetings. It introduces the problem and opens discussion of possible solutions.

The publicity manager coordinates the task of producing an AV presentation. Committee members and volunteers interested in writing, editing, and photographing should sign on to help.

The committee must first decide what type of AV presentation to produce. What will provide the most impact within the available budget of time, talent, and money?

The three main types are the scrapbook, the slide show, and the video. You can opt for any, all, or a combination of these.

THE SCRAPBOOK

Technically, the scrapbook is not an AV presentation. The audio part is missing, and it pretty much presents itself. It is simply a body of information collected in album or folder form.

A scrapbook is inexpensive to create. It is simple to assemble and revise. It is easy to carry around. It contains photographs with captions, drawings, maps, and data. Fact sheets containing more detailed information can be handed out as needed.

No special equipment or expertise is needed to use it. People can stop at any point to ask questions and discuss its contents.

But it lacks impact. Pictures are worth a thousand words, but without the sounds, the motion—the feel of the place—they are thin fare indeed.

Also a photo album is awkward to work with at meetings. It takes time to study it. Few people can look at it at once. If there is a crowd, many will not take the time (or will not have the time) to examine it. Those who are looking at the scrapbook are not paying attention to the rest of the presentation.

If you choose this option:

- Leave the scrapbook under wraps until the formal presentation is over. Otherwise, the audience will busy themselves poring over the scrapbook and neglect the speaker.
- The presenter must be ready to expand on any and all information included in the scrapbook: history and cost of old buildings, age and type of utilities, etc.
- Build several scrapbooks. They will take a beating during the focus group meetings and will need to be refreshed regularly. If more than one meeting is scheduled at a time, duplicates will be needed.

THE SLIDE SHOW

Another inexpensive option, a slide show is a series of pictures projected on a screen. The narrative is read by a live presenter or is recorded and timed to correspond to slide changes.

The slide show requires minimal equipment and technical know-how. It is easy to update and rearrange the slides and the narration.

Although better than a scrapbook, slides still lack the sound and motion— the life—of the school. Slides do not explain themselves. If the narrator is ill-prepared, or if the slide show is loaned out without an informed presenter, the script may be misread or lost. This reduces or destroys the impact of the presentation.

Another difficulty is interruptions from the audience. People feel freer to make comments and ask questions in the middle of a slide show. These pauses mitigate the impact, or worse, derail your presentation.

If you choose this option:

- Unlike the scrapbook, present the slides early in your program. This will focus the audience on the subject at hand and stimulate discussion.
- The slide show should last no more than 15 minutes. At its conclusion the audience should feel they haven't seen quite enough.
- Change subjects at least every 15 seconds. Avoid belaboring a single point. The slide show is an overview of school problems. It is not the place for detailed information.
- Show each slide for no longer than five or six seconds. If the narrative runs longer, choose several slides to illustrate the topic. Don't let a slide "stick" to the screen too long. Keep the show moving.
- To avoid confusion, be sure the narrative matches the slide on the screen.
- Let the narrative flow smoothly over the slide changes. Do not "block" the narrative to each slide. Avoid referring directly to the slide. "This is a view of . . ."
- The audience hears the narrative rather than reads it. Write the script for the ear, not for the eye.

The video section here contains additional advice that applies to slide shows, too.

THE VIDEO

Although slide shows or scrapbooks will do, a video is by far your best choice for an AV presentation. It more strongly captures the audience's attention and leaves less to the imagination. A well-designed video efficiently combines sight, sound, action, and facts. It shows more in less time. It engages more of the senses and brings the school to life for the viewers.

Almost everyone enjoys watching TV. It seems to captivate the audience. When people start watching a video, they generally sit through it to the end.

Here are three options for creating a video:

- You can shoot the video only and present it with live narration.
- You can shoot the video with live sound (what is actually being heard during filming) and narrate as you film.
- You can shoot the video with live sound then add narration during the editing phase.

MONEY, MONEY, MONEY . . .

The bad news about videos is that top-notch professional productions are very expensive. They can run up to $2,500 *per minute*. The good news is, you don't want a top-notch video.

Why not?

Even if you have deep pockets, it's too easy for people watching a glitzy production to wonder where the money came from to produce it. The opposition may try to use this point to distract from the video's purpose, which is to explain why the old school needs improvement.

Remember, you are a volunteer group working toward solving a community problem. Your goal is to produce a simple video, not a Hollywood movie.

The video should not be too slick nor should it be too amateurish. Fuzzy pictures or muffled sound will confuse and irritate the audience. Amateur efforts can produce sharp, well-exposed pictures and crisp sound. The technical aspect of your video should be as invisible as possible.

Where do you find a cameraman, writer, editor, and narrator at a price you can afford? Back to your committee . . .

Someone must know someone who knows someone in the AV business. Check around for a local professional who also may be a supporter. Ask him to volunteer to produce the video. At least ask the expert for free advice and suggestions. Mention that the video will be seen by practically everyone in town (you hope!) and the video company's name in the credits would be wonderful advertising.

If you have no luck finding a professional, the committee will just have to do it. All you need is a good quality video camera with sound capability, a shooting schedule, and a script. Good quality video recorders with sound are available at very reasonable prices. Surely someone on the committee owns one or knows a supporter who would be willing to loan one for this good cause. Put together a script and shooting schedule and you're on your way. Here is how it's done.

WHAT'S IN THE VIDEO?

The video should be no longer than about 15 minutes. This is the maximum attention span you can expect from your audience. The video will take your guests (the viewers) on a walking tour of the school. Assume the audience has never been inside the building. Even if you live in a small town where everyone attended the same school, it may be decades since some of the viewers have set foot inside it.

The purpose of the video is to highlight the shortcomings of the school. In it you will show the problems of health, safety, access, and overcrowding in each of the subject schools. Point out building age or poor design that leads to extra costs for maintenance, heating, and repair. Concentrate on inadequate classrooms and facilities used by the students. Compare them to state standards. Show how the lack of modern features frustrates education. Note conditions and floor plans that waste teachers' and students' time.

The video will show only the current situation and why improvement is needed. Its purpose is to show the problems, not to suggest specific solutions. Never let side issues creep into the video, such as the operating budget, personnel problems, or teaching methods.

HOW TO MAKE YOUR OWN SCHOOL VIDEO

The first step is to contact the school superintendent and the principal of each affected school. You will need their permission and cooperation to work within the school. Tell them the purpose of the video, which is to demonstrate to the community the need for improvement. Make it clear that you are not creating the video to scold or embarrass the school board, the administration, or the teachers. If you cannot show the voters why improvement is needed, the school bond will not get past the ballot box.

Ask the principal to take the AV task force on a thorough tour of the school(s). You will need full access to make the video—all classrooms, the furnace room, offices, utilities, the kitchen—everything.

The principal will know the shortcomings of his school. He can give you a priority list of areas that need improvement. Ask him to suggest topics that he would like brought to the public's attention.

Ask the principal to arrange a meeting for you with the teachers in the affected schools. They, of all people, will be able to direct you to the problems that make the school inefficient, unpleasant, and unsafe.

Explain your purpose to the teachers and ask for their comments and suggestions. Take careful notes. Don't allow the meeting to veer into side issues such as personalities, labor issues, or children with specific problems.

Now it's time to sit down and write the first draft of the script (see appendix B for script format). What do you want the public to know about the school's shortcomings? Which topics are most important? How much emphasis will you place on each?

Writing a script is different from writing a column or news release. It is written for the ear, not the eye. Write as you would speak. Grammatical errors are OK if they *sound* natural. Write in a lively manner. A stuffy or stilted style will put the audience to sleep. Use short, simple words in short, simple sentences. Even complex issues can be explained simply with careful word choice.

Next, read the draft aloud to the committee. Do not pass around copies. The audience will be listening to the narrative, not reading along with it. How does it sound?

Have you missed important points? Is any section confusing, too complicated, or belabored? Are the facts accurate? Complete?

Ask committee members, school administrators, and staff for comments and suggestions. Use this critique to add, cut, and hone the script to razor sharpness.

Develop a preliminary shooting schedule. Ask the principal to notify affected teachers and staff when to expect you. *Always* ask for permission before entering classrooms, offices, and utility areas.

Take a dry run of the shooting schedule. This consists of walking through the schedule without the camera. This rehearsal ensures there will be kids in the classroom or the library when you plan to be there. It confirms that the nurse will be in her office and the janitor will be around to open the furnace room for you. This is the time to work out the best camera angles.

Let everyone involved know when to expect you to return for the shoot. You will film during the school's normal class schedule.

Shooting day arrives. Count on spending at least a full day at each school.

The video must not be staged in any way. The video should show a typical day with no special events. Wherever possible, photograph students going about their normal activities. Ask teachers to instruct their students to ignore the camera. It is not uncommon for the opposition to accuse the video makers of faking school conditions to make them look worse.

Include as many kids in the video as possible. Parents and relatives will pay closer attention if there is a chance they'll spot their children on "TV." Avoid taking pictures of empty classrooms and deserted playgrounds. The children give the school life and realism. They drive home your point that the improvement is for the *children*—that crowding, outdated facilities, and health and safety hazards affect *children*.

Spend enough time on each shot to thoroughly cover the scene. Move the camera slowly. Take your time. Jumping around or swinging the camera too quickly will make the audience dizzy or disoriented.

If you are taping with live sound with a voice-over narrative, pay attention to the background noise. A loud motorcycle or jet aircraft sounds on the recording will distract and irritate your audience. The sounds must match what the audience is seeing. Make sure the background sounds don't over-power the message—unless your point is excessive noise at the school.

PUTTING IT ALL TOGETHER

Below are some tips to help you produce a successful video:

- The most important point to remember about the script is that it will be heard, not read. The style should be pleasant, conversational, and infor-mal.
- Make a strong introduction to grab your audience's attention and hold it. Let them know what they are about to see.
- Spell it out. Don't assume the audience has any prior knowledge of the school.
- The KISS principle (Keep it short, simple) is essential in AV presenta-tions. Your script must be lean and to the point. Use short words instead of fancy, long ones. Make your sentences short and simple. Good word choice can make complex issues easier to understand.
- Don't belabor a point or get bogged down in serious number crunching. If more explanation is needed, save it for the question-and-answer pe-riod or a handout.
- Choose active words. Don't beat around the bush.
- Perfect grammar? Forget all that. If a sentence fragment creates more impact, if it sounds better to the ear, use it.
- Be specific. Use facts and figures. But don't pack them too tightly.
- Where appropriate, let the background sounds of the kids and their school "do the talking." Don't bury your audience in words.
- There is nothing more boring than a "talking head," a person facing and talking to the camera. If a speaker must make a point on-screen, have him move about or demonstrate the point.

- Because the viewer cannot reread or review the video, repeat your most important points several times in different ways. For example, if the school's main problem is overcrowding, *show* crowded classrooms *and* a packed lunchroom *and* kids colliding on the tiny playground. *Tell* how much the student population exceeds the school's carrying capacity.
- Choose the narrator for his or her upbeat, pleasant voice. Or ask a local disk jockey or TV announcer to volunteer to narrate.
- Speak at around 100 words per minute. Don't rush, but keep it moving. Speak clearly and loudly enough to be heard.
- Don't dwell at length on any one problem. Keep it moving. Limit video scenes to around five or six seconds. As the point you are making runs over, change the camera angle or move to a related scene.
- Every statement you make needs pictures to illustrate it. For example, if you say the drop-off area is congested and dangerous, show a view of that area during "rush hour." If classrooms are overcrowded, film a classroom bulging with students.
- The words must closely match the pictures and live sounds. The audience will become confused if they hear one thing and see something unrelated.
- Do not date the video. If the bond fails on election day, the school problems will not go away. Design the video so it can be used again for another attempt. For example, don't say, "The school building is 84 years old and has not been renovated in 42 years." Instead say, "The school was built in 1913. It was last renovated in 1955."
- Don't be afraid to use a bit of humor or to throw something in to change the pace. These little nudges perk up the audience and sharpen their attention.
- The video should not threaten or badger the viewer or spread doom and gloom. Avoid melodrama. No one likes to be hit over the head. Simply show and tell the school situation as it is. If it is bad enough to warrant a school bond attempt, people will come to the right conclusion.
- The conclusion should wrap up your package in a neat little package by quickly restating your main points. Explain briefly why the audience should care.

Depending on your equipment, you might narrate as you shoot. This takes more preparation up-front because you must film exactly to the length of your prepared script. There is no room for error or changes. But it is simpler to do it this way.

Fancier cameras allow you to edit, cut, paste, and narrate over the sights and sounds of your video and add titles and captions. Either way, if you prepare well, you can create a perfectly adequate production for your needs.

You will want the video completed and ready to show toward the beginning of the education phase. It will be the centerpiece of the school bond effort right through the campaign.

A 15-minute video? That can't take too long to put together. Yes, it can! Producing a video is hard work. It will take *much* more time and effort than you expect. Start on it early.

But a picture truly is worth a thousand words. Add to the picture the sounds and atmosphere of the school, and you have a powerful tool in your bid for public awareness. An AV presentation is the most effective way to bring the community into the school. It will raise community awareness of the problems of the old school. It is well worth the effort.

Here is one final bit of advice. Set aside master copies of all AV items. Duplicate everything of importance—the video, slides, photo prints, the script. During the course of the school bond project, items will become lost or damaged. Don't get caught with nothing to show for your hard work.

7

Ambassadors Club

Before you can sell a person anything, you must make him want it more than the money it will cost.

Dan Poynter, author

TAKING YOUR MESSAGE TO THE PEOPLE

When you begin to talk about school improvement, you will discover that most people are much more interested in their quilting club, the World Series, or the latest video releases.

There is nothing wrong with any of these activities or with the countless other interests that make up the social fabric of a city or town. The school improvement committee simply has to make a place for itself among them. Taking the school situation directly to the people is crucial for success. Don't expect people to come to you. Chances are, most of them won't come.

Personal contact is the most productive method of education and persuasion. Meeting people face to face becomes particularly important if the media will not support your cause. If the newspaper, television, and radio ignore the school bond effort or, worse, oppose it, conducting focus group meetings is the most effective way to get your message to the voters.

This makes the ambassadors club one of the most important activities the committee will perform.

The goals of the ambassadors club are to:

• Bring the school's current condition to the public's attention.

- Convince citizens that there is a problem, that the problem is their own, and that everyone must work together to solve it.
- Alert people to what will happen if the problem is not addressed and solved.
- Make people aware of the benefits they'll receive for solving the problem. "What's in it for me."

The ambassadors club seeks out groups of people who focus on certain interests (hobby, profession, religion, etc.). Ambassadors make presentations to these groups, focusing on the school situation, hence the name, focus group meetings.

The ambassadors serve as a bridge bringing technical and financial information from the school board to the people and taking citizens' comments and suggestions back to the board. This helps the school board assess how people feel about the condition of the schools and how much the taxpayers will be willing to spend to improve it.

Ambassadors provide accurate information to group members who themselves become emissaries, spreading your message far and wide. If you are effective, every meeting produces a group of informed citizens, a handful of supporters, and a volunteer or two.

WHO ARE THE AMBASSADORS?

Unless you suffer from terminal stage fright, all committee members should serve as ambassadors. Interested volunteers and supporters also should be encouraged to join. The committee must screen potential ambassadors for pleasant personalities, organizational skills, and patience. This is not the place for the grumpy or short-tempered speaker.

The chief ambassador must have a lot of energy and stamina because this position and that of publicity manager are the two most strenuous and committed on the committee. Good people skills are a must, and experience in public speaking is a big plus. The chief ambassador must be ready to work for the committee over lunch, in the evenings and on weekends for the full duration of the project.

His duties will be to:

- Contact clubs and groups and schedule meetings
- Train ambassadors to conduct focus group meetings
- Assign ambassadors to focus group meetings

- Conduct many focus group presentations
- Work with the publicity manager to keep briefing books and handouts up-to-date
- Keep a log of meetings
- Follow through on unanswered questions, suggestions, and complaints

WHO IS THE AUDIENCE, AND WHERE DO YOU FIND THEM?

Your audience is anyone willing to listen, whenever and wherever you discover them. Start by identifying groups of voters by their professions, interests, activities, and age:

- *Parents and teachers:* They are directly affected by the school situation and the people most likely to vote for improvement. Contact the local parent-teacher organization, teachers' organizations, and school-related clubs (band boosters, sports clubs, etc.).
- *Business people:* Many are prominent members of the community. They are opinion leaders with high public exposure. If you can get them to support the bond, you are well on your way to success. Contact them through the chamber of commerce and various service organizations (Rotary, Lions, Jaycees, etc.). Ask to meet their employees over lunch.
- *Young adults:* They are less likely to be registered to vote but more likely to support school improvement. Their memory of school conditions is fresh. They may have strong feelings about the old school. They may influence their parents to vote for school improvement. Find copies of recent yearbooks or ask local high school(s) for lists of recent graduates. Search out college organizations and athletic clubs (adult league soccer and baseball). Don't forget current high school seniors. They have opinions on school issues, and many are eligible to vote.
- *Religious leaders and their congregations:* If people are active in church affairs, it is likely they are active in other civic functions.
- *Social or service clubs:* Many members are interested in community growth and progress and will understand the value of modern, attractive schools (Optimist, American Legion, Elks, etc.).
- *Hobby clubs:* These are very diverse groups with a broad range of interests (antique fanciers, wood carvers, historical society, etc.).
- *Seniors:* In small towns, seniors make up a large part of the population. Many elderly people live on fixed incomes. As a group, unless convinced otherwise, they will vote to keep taxes down. They can be a

tough group to sell your idea to. Many older folks are less mobile. They are less likely to have visited the school(s) recently and are not likely to come to you for information. But they resent being ignored. Make a special effort to visit them where they gather. Seek them out at senior centers and clubs.

- *Others:* Cultural groups, chamber of commerce members, professionals (doctors, attorneys), political leaders, and realtors, for example, should be contacted. Wherever people congregate, there is a group for you to talk to.

How do you find these groups, clubs, and the like? A committee brainstorming session should get you started. Each committee member will have at least one affiliation of some kind: band booster, swim team parent, a member of a church or social group, a business affiliation, or a hobby club.

Call the local chamber of commerce. They will have lists of area businesses and their members and probably of local service organizations.

Ask spouses, neighbors, and relatives for suggestions. Each person has a network of associations and interests. Don't confine yourselves to only school and child-related groups. Non-parents are voters, too!

Newspapers often include a section listing social and support groups and club meetings.

Let those fingers walk through the phone book.

Don't neglect groups of obvious supporters. You may feel "preaching to the choir" is a waste of time, but it would be a mistake to pass them by. If you provide supporters with accurate, up-to-date information, you inspire them to spread your message.

It should not be too hard for ambassadors to get invited to speaking engagements. Clubs and organizations are always looking for speakers to present timely issues.

If possible, assign an ambassador to present to groups and organizations in which he is a member. Everyone involved starts out on a more familiar, friendly note, and it saves time on introductions.

PREPARING TO MEET THE PUBLIC

The chief ambassador is responsible for training the ambassadors. If the chief is not well versed in public speaking or sales, ask the local Toastmasters International group for advice and help. Recruit a local speech or debate teacher as a coach to provide expert training.

No one becomes good at any activity without practice. Ambassadors should rehearse together before they venture into the focus group meetings.

Ask each other "tough" questions. Get unreasonable. Irritate one another. Rebut negative arguments. Critique each performance. The more you practice, the more confident you will become. The more focus group meetings you conduct, the easier they get.

Decide on what you plan to say to all groups. The crux of your pitch to each type of focus group must be the same; otherwise, you may be accused of "telling people what they want to hear." But it is perfectly all right to adapt your presentation style to the age and interests of each group.

Prepared as you are, you can count on making mistakes. You will learn from them and improve with every meeting.

Organize the formal part of your presentation to last no more than 30 minutes. This includes the introduction, stating the problem, showing the audiovisual presentation, and reporting current developments and activities. The more informal question and discussion period that follows will no doubt run later. People who are not interested or have time constraints will be free to leave.

How big should the groups be? Keep them small, ideally no more than 15 people. (Of course, if 50 Rotarians show up at a meeting, go ahead and make your presentation!)

Why? Generally, the larger the group, the less feedback you will get. Many people, ambassadors and audience alike, would rather die than speak in public. People usually feel less reluctant to look stupid in front of 10 friends than 50 strangers. The smaller the group, the more likely each member of the audience will feel obligated to speak up. Big groups provide prime targets for the occasional person who likes to "grandstand" on a soap box. Finally, it's easier to save face with a small group following a foolish remark or off night than to make a fool of yourself in front of half the town!

Two committee members should attend each meeting. One will actually conduct the meeting, the other will record comments, help set up and run the audiovisual presentation, distribute handouts, and circulate a sign-up sheet for supporters and volunteers. Ambassadors-in-training can start out as recording ambassadors.

Arrive early. Have everything set up and working well before the group arrives. Know where the light switches are. Ensure your audiovisual presentation is set to begin. Make sure the sound system (if needed) is working. This shows your audience basic good manners and respect. Never keep them waiting.

Keep the formal presentation within your allotted time limit. Don't make people late to work or to other appointments.

Show up at the meeting well groomed. Dress simply, but well. Dress so your clothing does not distract from your message. Don't wear clanking jewelry, overly bold patterns, or rustling material.

Hold the meeting in a small room if possible. This brings you closer to your audience. In smaller quarters it is easier to put the group at ease and get them to relax.

Set up the chairs in a semicircle or in small groups around tables. Avoid ranking the chairs in neat little rows. Tidy, straight lines stifle creativity and ease.

Avoid podiums and microphones. They isolate you from the group. Walk around. Tell a few jokes. Briefly ask about the interests of the group.

Bring a flip chart to the meeting. A flip chart serves two purposes. First, you can write questions and facts or draw diagrams on it beforehand to guide and focus the discussion. Second, the recording ambassador can write down the suggestions, comments, and criticisms coming from the group. This clarifies and distills comments. It shows that you are listening and that you understand and care about the group's concerns. People like to see evidence that their comments are being taken seriously. They like to "see it in writing." However, don't let the mechanics of writing on a flip chart slow down the meeting's momentum.

The recording ambassador also must write down all the promises people make, the names of potential volunteers and committee members, questions that cannot be answered, and the people you say you will get back to later. Follow through.

HOW TO CONDUCT A FOCUS GROUP MEETING

Think of yourself as a salesman. The way you deliver your pitch is at least as important as the message itself. People buy people. They will be buying you as a representative of the committee and the school issue. It is much easier to get someone to agree with you if they like you and feel you are similar to themselves.

Make yourself attractive to your audience by being friendly and sincere. Make constant eye contact with the audience. Compliment them, but avoid crass flattery. Impress upon them that you respect their opinions. You can't fake this!

Select your words carefully. Speak the language of the audience. Don't talk up or down to them. Use positive, active words and images whenever possible.

Make your presentation with enthusiasm, confidence, and conviction. Assure the audience that you know your "product" (school improvement) and firmly stand behind it.

Be a good listener. After your formal presentation is over, encourage your audience to offer their comments, questions, and opinions. Let them do most of the talking. Listen attentively without interrupting. The members of the focus group need to feel they are being heard and understood. Pause before responding to direct questions. Answering too fast gives the impression you didn't hear or don't care about the comments.

Be concise, factual, and logical. Get to the point and collect the audience's response to that point. Then move on to the next point. The average adult attention span is somewhere around 15 minutes. Put that prime time to good use.

Be flexible. If discussion takes an unexpected but promising turn, go with it. Look for openings on the new tangent to state your case. But do not become sidetracked from the subject. This wastes everyone's time.

Don't be pushy. Always respond calmly. Don't let your tone of voice block your message. Be cool, calm, focused, and relaxed.

Begin the meeting by thanking everyone for coming. Praise the audience for caring about such an important issue. Introduce yourself. Clearly explain your specific goals for the meeting—why you are there and what you expect to accomplish. You are there to discuss a mutual problem. Your common goal is to work together toward a solution.

Introduce your partner, the recording ambassador, and explain that he will be taking careful notes of all suggestions and advice. This information will be forwarded to the committee and the school board.

Request that questions be held, as they may be answered during the formal presentation.

Show the AV presentation, either slide show or video. This opens the subject by stating the problem. If you have only a scrapbook, save it until the end of the meeting.

After the video or slide show, kindly but firmly establish ground rules for the discussion period. For example:

- Discussion will be restricted to school facility issues (not teaching, administrative issues, or the sports program).
- You will not discuss other community problems, such as potholes, congestion, or crime—even if it is related to the school.
- To keep the meeting orderly, request that each person wishing to comment raise his hand. Ask that each speaker be allowed to say his piece without interruption.

- Request that people keep their comments brief and to the point so everyone will have a chance to speak.
- Request that comments be directed to the ambassador, not to each other. This will prevent heated exchanges between people of strongly differing opinions. It keeps the meeting from spinning out of your control.
- If discussion is slow to get started, you might ask a series of questions to loosen them up (see later). Probe for the groups' feelings and ideas about the school situation. Encourage the group by saying that all opinions are valuable.

Openly accept negative comments along with the positive ones. They get to the heart of resistance to school improvement. The committee will have to address these issues if the school bond is to be successful. It's better to face them than have them muttered behind your back.

Allow all participants to have their say. If you allow the group to express objections thoroughly, you clear the path to consensus. Venting takes the wind out of sails and leaves potential opponents more receptive to your message. But try to rein in rambling, repeating, or straying off the main subject.

Don't argue. You are there to address a problem, not pick a fight. The audience will "clam up" or "overheat" if you contradict them. Stress points of mutual agreement, not conflict. Try to find at least some point of a negative opinion to agree with. For instance, to a negative statement about the cost you might respond, "You're right, building a new school is a major investment for a community of this size . . ." Then make your pitch.

Close your presentation with a call to action.

HOW TO HANDLE A TOUGH CROWD

Most focus group meetings will be cordial. You will receive a courteous welcome, and a civil discussion will follow. Even groups that mostly disagree with you will be polite.

But occasionally an opponent or opponents will try to stampede the meeting and thwart open discussion. What do you do if a noisy opponent or faction tries to hijack the meeting?

Be polite but maintain firm control. Never answer a mean, sarcastic, personal, or insulting comment in kind. Be cool and pleasant, even if someone is working hard to make you lose your temper.

To cool a heated atmosphere, slowly restate the negative statement(s), even if they are shouted at you. This slows the pace a bit and allows everyone time to calm down. It also shows you are listening carefully, understand, and are taking the concerns seriously.

Look for common ground. Impress upon the aggressor(s) that you are not adversaries but allies searching for the best solution to a common problem. Work hard to turn negative remarks to your advantage.

For example, "I see your point. Taxes are high, and there isn't much we can do about them. But unlike state or federal taxes, a school bond is part of local taxes for which you will see local benefits . . ." or "I understand your concern about the cost of a new school. What will happen if we continue to put this off?"

Try to soften opposition by asking the group to make positive suggestions. "Shall we bat around some alternatives? An addition, renovation, or repair?" This often derails and exposes naysayers because they have no alternatives. Ask for more specifics to find out the reason for criticism.

Be prepared to answer the "no action" choice with solid facts and figures. Explain why continuing the current school situation is not in their best interest.

Allow everyone a chance to comment, but politely shut down each speaker after a suitable amount of time. "Thanks for your comments. You've expressed that point of view very well. Now, who hasn't had a chance to speak?" If a showboat persists on trying to dominate the discussion, thank him again, remind the group there are many subjects to cover and invite him to stay after the meeting to explore his issue further.

If tempers begin to flare, do what you can to lower the temperature. Cut off debate for a moment. Remind the group of the ground rules. Ask everyone to stand and stretch.

If comments begin to slip into the personal, mean, or nasty zone, ask your host to police or discipline those disrupting the meeting. You do not have to tolerate rudeness or insults.

What if the worst happens and, despite your best effort, the meeting spins completely out of control? When the first live skunk comes flying your way, calmly and politely pack up and leave. If a few hotheads deny you the chance to exchange ideas in a civil manner, there is nothing to be gained by prolonging the meeting. It wastes everyone's time.

It can be hard to do, but the committee will gain stature if the ambassadors can remain cheerful and pleasant in the face of adversity. You will be seen as the underdog—the nice guest who was attacked by your hosts. After the meeting, some embarrassed group members may apologize for the aggressors' behavior. This gives you a chance to be gracious and ask them to consider your ideas.

What if you know beforehand that you have been invited into the "lion's den," say the Tax-haters League? You know the audience will be hostile, and you don't want the meeting to turn into a row or a roast. How can you turn a negative group to your advantage?

Think positively. Negative comments are golden opportunities. By addressing them in the open, you can provide accurate facts and figures and clear up misconceptions and rumors. Bringing murky subjects into the light can cut down on the "whispering campaign" that so often starts with these groups. If you remove the props under some of the negative arguments, you reduce the strength of the opposition.

To prevent yourself from being steamrolled, go in prepared to "divide and conquer."

Before the meeting begins, arrange the chairs around tables. If tables are not available, cluster chairs in small separate groups.

Compile worksheets and discussion material into identical packets. Each packet's top sheet should be one of several colors. Pass out the packets at the door as people arrive for the meeting. If several people arrive together, be sure each person gets a different color packet.

After your initial remarks and the audiovisual presentation, divide the audience into small groups, one color for each cluster or table. Give the audience a constructive assignment and a time limit to complete it. The green group, for example, might be asked to list possible locations for the school (current location, north of town, on the old football field) and the pros and cons for each. The yellow group's task might be to examine alternatives for school facility improvement (addition, renovation, new school). The ambassador circulates among the groups, encouraging and clarifying each assignment.

Splitting the audience this way breaks up cliques and gives troublemakers something productive to do.

At the end of the breakout session, bring everyone back together. Ask one member of each cluster to report to the whole group. Log all responses on the flip chart.

Most focus group discussions will be civil, pleasant experiences. But negative meetings do happen. Heated conflicts aren't fun. Go to every meeting dressed in your "rhino skin" and radiating good humor and confidence.

Remember, opponents seldom resent you personally, just your message.

FOCUS GROUP TIMING

And what is your message? The theme carried to focus group meetings corresponds to the phase of the school bond effort:

The *information phase* starts at the same time as the phone survey. Ambassadors probe community attitudes and perceptions of the current school situation. Is improvement needed? If so, what type? At this stage, the focus groups toss around ideas and suggestions. This is when you test the waters for support of a school bond. The committee's stance in this phase is totally neutral.

During the *education phase*, ambassadors inform the public of the short-comings of the old facilities and explore alternatives for school improvement. This is the time to search for consensus. Inform the public of the latest school board developments. The committee may declare its support for a school bond, but it remains strictly impartial about alternatives.

For the *campaign phase*, ambassadors drop neutrality and "sell" the bond proposal that the school board has adopted. The board will provide the committee with specific models, drawings, and costs for the proposal. The ambassadors will display and explain the design and scope of the project. This information is of vital concern to voters.

At every phase, the ambassadors identify supporters and volunteers for the school bond effort. In the final phase, these supporters become the "yes" voters who are encouraged to go to the polls on election day.

Try to make multiple visits to each group. Ideally you will contact every group once during each phase. During the last few weeks before the election, your efforts will intensify. Try to contact as many of the groups as you can with a final pitch.

WHAT TO TAKE TO THE MEETING

Ambassadors go to focus group meetings equipped with more than a smile. Your bag of tricks includes the following for each phase of the meeting:

Information Phase

- Flip chart to record comments and suggestions and pen and paper to list supporters and volunteers
- Introductory list of questions (see later for ideas)
- Copies of focus group survey
- Briefing book containing history of past school bond attempts and election results

Education Phase

Take all of the just-listed items except the survey, plus the following:

- Video/TV monitor/VCR or slide projector/screen or photo album illustrating why improvements are needed
- Briefing book will now include facts and figures on the current school situation: classroom size, wiring, acreage, cost of maintenance, facility weaknesses, etc.
- Handouts covering pros/cons of site or design options. Handouts will be up-to-date and appropriate.

Campaign Phase

All of the previously listed are needed plus the following:

- Signature poster (see chapter 11, The Campaign)
- Campaign ribbons, buttons, signs, etc.
- Voter registration cards
- School design or model
- Campaign brochure
- Briefing book will now include information on design features of the proposed school, facts and figures on cost, location, size, acreage, and whatever is relevant to the project

SUGGESTED FOCUS GROUP QUESTIONS

Every focus group will be different. Most people, however, will wait for you, standing up there in front, to make the first move. Below is a list of questions that might help prime the audience for the question-and-answer period.

- How many of you are registered voters?
- How many have children in school? Grandchildren?
- Have you lived in town a long time? Short time?
- Have you visited the school facilities recently?
- How do the school facilities here compare with other schools you have seen or experienced?
- Do you feel it is time for a change in the school facilities?
- Could you support school improvement? What would it take to gain your support?
- What would ideal school facilities be like?
- (Include a brief synopsis of past successful and failed bond issues.) Why do you think this bond issue(s) failed/succeeded?

- What did you like about the last (un)successful bond proposal?
- What do you feel it would take for the community to support a bond issue?
- Is the location of the school an important factor?
- If a new school were built, where do you feel the best site would be? (List several site options.) Which do you prefer? Why?
- Do you prefer renovating (expanding) the old school?
- Do you know what it would cost you per month if a school bond issue passed? (Provide estimated costs when available.)
- If you voted "no" in any previous school bond elections, why?
- Did you feel you received enough information about past bond issues to make an informed decision? If not, what was missing?

While the telephone survey is underway, ask the focus group members to fill out a survey. You can use the same forms the phone pollsters use. Even though they may be contacted by phone, completing the survey at the focus group meeting allows people more time to write comments and suggestions.

OUTLINE FOR CONDUCTING PRESENTATIONS

(Again, this is just to get you thinking.)

   I. Introduce yourself and other committee members present, and state the specific goal of the meeting.
  II. Demonstrate the problem by showing the video or slide show (education and campaign phases) and make the disclaimer that nothing shown in the video, slides, or photos was staged, rigged, or misrepresented.
 III. Make a short, concise pitch, depending on the phase of your project.
   A. Information phase: Bat around ideas, get a feel for community's attitude. Do they perceive a problem with current school situation? Offer participants a chance to take a survey.
   B. Education phase: Discuss current problems and various proposed solutions. Mention maintenance costs, upcoming repairs, government-mandated upgrades to old building(s). Seek consensus.
   C. Campaign phase: Describe bond proposal.
     1. How final design was reached? By whom?

    2. Provide a cost breakdown: cost, bond length, tax levy.

    3. Give a tour of school model or floor plan.

    4. Solicit active support for the bond.

IV. Hold an open discussion and comments session.

  A. Why not wait for a more favorable time?

    1. Costs will only go up.

    2. The old school is getting older and more expensive to repair and maintain.

    3. It puts our children at an educational disadvantage.

    4. It discourages community growth and is embarrassing.

    5. Current health, safety, and access regulations must be addressed.

  B. "What's in it for me?"

    1. There will be improved educational quality and opportunity for the children.

    2. The new/improved school will be attractive to businesses.

    3. It will create community pride.

  V. Announce upcoming events.

  A. Talk about committee-sponsored activities/events.

  B. Address the need for volunteers.

  C. Restate election day and polling locations (campaign phase).

VI. Distribute voter registration cards to non-registered voters (campaign phase).

VII. Pass around signature poster (see chapter 11, The Campaign).

VIII. Distribute handouts.

  A. Make a sign-up sheet for volunteers.

  B. Include informational handouts (education phase) and/or brochures (campaign phase).

  C. Give out campaign ribbons, literature, yard signs, etc. (campaign phase).

  D. Display the photo album (if this is your audiovisual material).

IX. Hang around for informal discussion.

This is a lot of ground to cover in a very short time. Keep the meeting moving and on track. Don't become bogged down on any one subject or with any one person.

Save handouts until the end of the meeting so members of the group don't fiddle with them and stop paying attention to you. One can only hope that the handouts will be taken home to be read at leisure and shared with spouses, colleagues, and friends.

The pro/con sheet can be very effective if not overdone. It will change with circumstances and the phase of your project. It must be brief and to the point and no more than a single page (see appendix B). A long, dense handout will seldom be read.

In the education phase it will compare the advantages and disadvantages of various sites or designs. The final handout will be the campaign brochure, which will include information on the design and cost of the bond and the reasons why the voters should approve it.

IT'S NOT OVER UNTIL THE PAPERWORK'S DONE

At each weekly committee meeting, all focus group comments and survey forms will be turned over to the survey-canvass coordinator. Give the secretary-treasurer the names of all identified supporters and volunteers.

Ambassadors should make a brief report to the committee after each focus group meeting. This allows the entire committee to feel the pulse of the community. The report airs citizens' concerns the committee may not have thought of and helps the chief ambassador and publicity manager to add, alter, delete, or tighten presentation materials.

It helps the publicity manager pinpoint rumors and misinformation to be addressed through the media. It exposes gaps in public awareness.

The report also identifies opponents and their arguments. The report asks the unanswered questions so accurate follow-up calls can be made.

Finally, consider sending a note to the group or club thanking it for the opportunity to present your information. This is a nice touch and one more positive contact.

Focus group presentations are works in progress. Strive to continuously fine-tune and improve them.

TOWN HALL MEETING: THE ULTIMATE FOCUS GROUP

A town hall meeting can be the biggest focus group of all. You will receive a lot of media coverage. Many people will come to see what the project is all about.

But is arranging a big public meeting the right thing to do? Will you gain enough publicity to make it worthwhile? Will increasing community awareness gain you support or fan the flames of opposition?

Is the opposition mean, strong, organized, and articulate? Is there a chance that your opponents might hijack the meeting?

These are important questions for the committee to consider before planning a town hall meeting.

If your presentation is overwhelmed in a focus group meeting, you have lost only a small debate. In a town hall meeting, a few strong, well-placed opponents can make it appear the whole audience is against you. At worst, it could cost you the election.

IN CONCLUSION

The purpose of focus group meetings is to make the public aware there is a problem, that it is everyone's problem, and to search for a solution.

There are five ironclad rules to follow at every focus group meeting:

1. *Keep it simple.* Make your presentation short and concise. People are chronically overloaded with choices and demands on their time. Let's face it, your whole effort is just one more sales pitch—an effort to get the public to "buy" a school bond. As with any sales call, if you overwhelm the audience with information, their eyes will glaze over and you will lose them. Be thoroughly prepared to provide details, but avoid burying the audience with them.
2. *Always tell the truth.* Your credibility is your greatest asset. If you lose that, you are wasting your time. Once lost, you will never get it back.
3. *Don't get sidetracked.* Topics related but outside the scope of your committee's work (teachers' salaries or problems with curriculum or personalities) waste time and dilute your message. You are working for the kids to improve school facilities.
4. *Stay cool.* Conduct all meetings in a calm, friendly manner. The ambassador's objective is to shed light on the subject, not set fire to it.
5. *Follow through.* If you don't know the answer to a question, never try to "wing it" or make something up. Respond, "I don't know, but I'll find out and get back to you with an accurate answer by tomorrow." Then follow through.

Ambassadors must be ready for the long haul. Taking your message directly to the people will be one of the committee's first, last, and most important tasks. To do it well is to take a giant step toward success.

8

Special Interests, Special Issues

*The whole people must take upon themselves the education of the whole
people—and must be willing to bear the expense of it.*

John Adams, U.S. president

A community is a group of people living in the same place organized around
a set of common interests. As the poet John Donne said, "No man is an is-
land entire of itself . . ." Within each community, nearly everyone is linked
by a web of friends, associates, neighbors, and coworkers. People join clubs,
teams, and congregations. They won't agree entirely on everything, but
members generally share similar interests and opinions.

Conversely, each community has its own unique mix of priorities, problems, and prejudices. Each has its own school situation, and each school has
its own set of problems.

To most effectively take its message to the community, the committee
must identify the various groups. Then the ambassadors must contact as
many of these groups as possible. From these visits, the committee will determine what the public perceives as the greatest school problems. The committee will also gauge the limit of each group's support for various options.

You're in luck if the school district and the people generally agree on the
areas of greatest need. But keep in mind, the public and the district may have
two very different sets of priorities.

Beware. To ignore the people's *feelings* in favor of logical school district
needs is to invite defeat.

ARGUMENTS AND RESPONSES

Below are listed several groups of people and possible approaches to take with each. This will be followed by a list of special situations and issues and how the committee might deal with them. The more negative groups will be discussed in chapter 9, Opposing Views.

Parents

"I already plan to vote 'yes' for a school bond. Believe me, I know what awful shape that old school is in."

Parents of school-age children are generally the strongest supporters of school improvement. They are most directly informed and involved in school affairs. They, through their children, have the most at stake.

You may be tempted to neglect asking them for their support, assuming their "yes" votes are already in the ballot box. To take them for granted would be a big mistake for two reasons.

First, loaded with accurate information, parent-supporters serve as active advocates for the bond. They spread the word by talking to friends, neighbors, and associates who may not be parents. Hearing the facts from a personal acquaintance can have much more impact than hearing them from a member of the committee.

Second, this group is fertile ground from which to recruit volunteers. Not only do they spread the word, they also spread the work. Besides, each active volunteer is a committed "yes" vote. The more the merrier.

Approach this group through as many school activities as you can find: parent-teacher organization (PTO) meetings, youth activities, clubs, or sports. Ask the PTO if an ambassador may give progress reports of the committee's efforts at monthly meetings. Send ambassadors to the band boosters meeting. Buttonhole soccer parents at the games.

Make sure the committee is listed on the agenda for each scheduled school board meeting. Present a short progress report to the board. Add a little pep talk. Not only does this keep the board informed of your activities and progress, but board meetings are public. The newspaper carries accounts of the meetings, and your monthly report will reach a wider audience.

Non-Parents or Parents of Grown Children

"My kids are grown. I don't really care about school issues anymore."

In 1950, near the start of the "Baby Boom," the U.S. population was around 151 million. It seemed everyone was having kids and lots of them. School bonds passed left and right, as nearly everyone saw the need for new modern schools.

Although the U.S. population today approaches 300 million, there are fewer children per household. Thus, today's voters are less likely to have children in school or they have fewer children in school for a shorter span of time.

Those without children in school are less directly involved with the schools. They are less aware of school problems and needs and have less sympathy for them.

How do you convince voters out of touch with school affairs that the condition of the school affects their quality of life? How do you reach them and convince them that school improvement is in their best interest?

Everyone should be made aware of the value of a vibrant school system. Modern, well-equipped schools are attractive to top job applicants who are also parents. Many service jobs are held by younger people who have school-age children.

For homeowners, a good school can make a neighborhood more attractive. By preserving or raising the value of their real estate, homeowners are protecting the worth of what is for many their biggest financial investment.

Good schools lead the list of amenities that every town strives for. They encourage people to settle in the community. Poor schools encourage people to take their families (and jobs and money) to another town.

Seniors

"I'm retired, just getting by. I can't afford to have my taxes raised."

The elderly can be the least supportive voting bloc of school bond initiatives. Seniors are usually retired and living on fixed incomes. They worry that an increase in taxes will squeeze them financially. And they do vote.

Many states give property tax breaks to homeowners aged 65 years and older. If your state provides this tax break for seniors, make sure they are aware of this and understand how it affects their taxes should the school bond pass.

Render the tax increase of the proposed bond in bite-size pieces. Compare it to the cost of a daily cup of coffee or a candy bar. This takes some of the sting out of it and brings it more down to a human scale.

"I've already paid to have my kids educated. Why should I have to pay to educate strangers?"

The old saw goes, the only sure things are death and taxes. How do you convince seniors that, although they may be retired, they have neither retired from life nor from their obligation to their community?

Remind seniors of the sacrifices shouldered by their forefathers in providing them with school facilities. Now is the time for today's seniors to provide for future generations.

Does the community support a senior center? Does the community help fund senior services and activities? Point out these commitments to seniors (in a positive way, of course) as an example of people helping each other.

Emphasize the strong connection between the seniors' well-being and the health of the schools. Point out how good schools benefit them directly— professionals and competent service employees who are parents of school-age children. Can one neglect the other?

"That school was good enough for me and my kids. It should be good enough for today."

It may be decades since the seniors last set foot inside the old school, or they may have been educated elsewhere. Some may be nostalgic about the old school and resist seeing it replaced.

Others might not be aware of developments in education that require upgrades in facilities, equipment, and curriculum.

Organize a special open house of the school facilities for all the community's senior citizens. Organize a "seniors day" or "grandparents day" at the school. Make them a special invitation they can't refuse. Ply them with food and entertainment by the students.

Give tours of the facility. Point out the inadequacies of the old buildings and how much education has evolved.

If they can't or won't go, take the video or slide presentation to the seniors. Highlight the shortcomings of the school and its special needs.

Personalize the school situation. When was the last time some of these seniors came face to face with a cute kid? Organize children's musical programs at the senior center. Have the kids draw pictures or write stories for the seniors.

Many elderly people do not get out much. Go out of your way to take your road show to them. Send ambassadors to the senior center, church gatherings, small bridge parties, and quilting or antique club meetings.

Be extra patient and relaxed with the elderly. Concentrate on the personal touch. Because of hearing loss and slower reflexes, seniors may find it more difficult to assimilate information. Present your information clearly and thoroughly.

But never sound patronizing! Seniors have been around long enough to detect condescension a mile away.

As election day approaches, help elderly supporters apply for absentee ballots if they cannot get to the polls in person. If transportation will be a problem, arrange rides for them on election day.

Private School Patrons

"My kids don't even go to that school, and I'm paying for it anyway. Why should I support raising my taxes for no benefit?"

The more students in the district who attend parochial or other private schools, the harder it will be to pass a school bond. The smaller the district, the more impact the private school will have.

The public/private school issue is emotionally charged. It often leads to hard feelings before, during, and after a school bond effort.

Very few people involved with a non-public school—parents, grandparents, parishioners—will publicly admit that they plan to vote "no" in a school bond election. But the fact is, people generally vote their own best interests.

Why should someone vote to raise his taxes for something from which he receives little benefit? On the other hand, how can someone in good conscience vote to deny a decent school for his neighbor's children?

How do you reach voters with children in private school?

First, track down all the issues, fears, and grudges relating to the two (or more) school systems. Who are the major patrons and leaders in the private structure? What are their opinions on public school improvement? Do administrators and parents of the private school fear they will lose students to the shiny new public school? Look for ways to reassure them.

Can you find supporters among them who have kids attending the non-public schools? Recruit them to the committee. They are the best ambassadors to meet with these special groups.

Sponsor events that will include *all* the kids in town. Make sure students from the private schools feel welcome. Go to great lengths to avoid a "them versus us" image.

Do the school systems share academic, special education, or sports programs? Do the schools share facilities or a hot lunch program? Emphasize this cooperation in a positive light. It is natural that private school patrons might fear losing joint programs if the bond passes. Find ways to reassure them that they will not lose ground.

The committee should be willing to act as liaison between the school systems. Begin shuttle diplomacy between the school boards early in the process. Ask each private school board if a committee representative can attend regularly scheduled meetings to report the committee's progress. Be prepared to carry messages among the various boards. Nail down agreements, and get them in writing. Have the boards spell everything out. Don't assume anything.

If rumors begin to crackle and fly, knock them down with straightforward, accurate information. Keep those lines of communication open. Work hard for harmony and good will. You won't win without it.

DIFFERENT STROKES FOR DIFFERENT FOLKS

If the community is ethnically or culturally diverse, the committee must make a special effort to include every group in the school bond process. Recruit committee members, ambassadors, and volunteers from every group so no one feels neglected or excluded.

If possible, send ambassadors to speak to ethnic groups in their native languages. Spell out how the new school will benefit the *entire* community. Emphasize the benefits of a new or improved school to *all* the children.

Provide campaign literature in the languages most represented. Create special mailings targeted specifically for the various ethnic voting blocs. Develop a special outreach program so residents understand the issues and the voting process. Make a special effort to register ethnic supporters to vote.

SPECIAL ISSUES

There are special issues that also can complicate a school bond referendum. Here are a few and how to deal with them.

New School Site

Many a bond has gone down in flames because the voters did not like the site chosen.

Proposing to build a new school and abandon the old can be very upsetting to settled towns with only one or two schools. Many people will nostalgically oppose a move, even though the old site is totally inappropriate for modern education and the long term.

If a new school site might be a problem in your community, make sure to probe this issue on your original survey and in focus group meetings during the education phase.

Organize a panel to carefully study all possible sites. The panel should consist of members of the committee, the school board, the architect, the city engineer, and anyone who might be interested. Make sure *everyone* is invited to join the panel. Chances are few people will show up, but at least offer the public the chance to participate.

Carefully examine each site, pro and con, and try to reach a consensus. Study each with your brain and your heart. Logic is all well and good, but it may not win a school bond election. The committee must be very sensitive to how the voters will *feel* about each proposed site.

Example: The best site by far for the new school is a field near the center of town with plenty of room. The only hitch is that a major electric transmission line runs through the middle of it.

Choosing that site will be nothing but trouble. Why?

Many people worry about the health hazard of electromagnetic fields. You can pile health studies as high as the power poles pointing to the harmlessness of electric current, but people will resist that site.

Example: The most promising site adjoins a drug rehabilitation center. The center has been there for 25 years with not a single problem. But the voters may shy away anyway, worried about contact through the fence between "those people" and their children.

Example: The most logical site includes what is now the high school football field. Hardly anyone will admit it, but this is hallowed ground of past glory. It is loaded with emotional baggage.

There will always be resistance to placing a new school on the edge of town. But this is often where adequate space is available. If the best site for a new school would be on the edge of town, try to locate it in the natural direction of growth.

Another problem with relocating a school to the edge of town is the increased distance many students will have to travel to school. This is a particularly thorny issue for relocating an elementary school.

One way around it is to ask teachers to conduct a survey of their students in each class. Provide a standard form for the survey so you get consistent data (see appendix D).

How many students walk to school daily? How many times per week? Do they walk home from school? How often? How many get rides to and from school?

The results may surprise you. Very few children today walk any distance to school on a regular basis. Most get rides from parents, relatives, or friends or take the bus. Would enough children be affected adversely to arouse serious opposition? Publish the survey results.

If it is a very long distance from the farthest boundary to the proposed new school site, the school board must prepare a busing plan *before* the election. If buses are already used, the school board must prepare a revised plan, so parents will know whether their children will be riding the bus.

Can the school schedule be rearranged to allow parents to drop off their kids on their way to work? Can an after-school program be developed to keep kids safely learning or playing at school until parents can pick them up?

The school board should work out solutions to these issues *before* the bond is placed before the voters.

Community Growth

Is yours a fast-growing community? This is good news for school bond success. A sudden large increase in student enrollment often leads to solid approval of bond issues for two reasons.

First, the need to alleviate crowding is a strong and obvious reason to build a new school or to increase the size of an old one. It is hard to ignore overcrowding or argue against relieving it.

The committee should emphasize public awareness of the problem. Many voters have not been inside school buildings since the day they walked out with diplomas in hand. Offer guided tours of the school while it is in session. Emphasize overcrowding in focus group meetings and in your audiovisual presentation.

Second, with population growth comes an expanding tax base. The tax increase produced by bond passage will be spread out among more taxpayers. This is easy for the voters to understand—*if* you make them aware of it.

Poor Community with Declining Tax Base

This can be a desperate situation because declining enrollment often leads to bond failure. In isolated rural towns, when people complain they can't afford it, they are probably right.

But if school improvement does not occur, more people will move away, worsening the situation. In the smallest towns, if the school fails to thrive, the town may dwindle as well.

How do you convince a poor declining community to increase its taxes for a new or improved school?

Engage as many people as possible as early as you can in the planning process. Concentrate on making the school design as lean as possible. Voters must be convinced that the improvement is truly needed and that there is no fat in the proposal.

Instead of adding to or replacing an old school, consider linking several schools electronically. This allows a few students from each school to attend the same class at the same time through the Internet, satellite links, and multiple-site interactive television connections. These options reduce isolation and share scarce resources among schools in the district and with other districts. Distance learning is a bit more expensive than traditional classes, but many more classes can be offered without commuting. It is cheaper than building a new school.

Check with the state education department on possible grants for distance education. Philanthropic organizations are also good prospects for matching funds.

If interactive linkage can be incorporated in the bond asking, this can be a strong incentive for bond passage. The public must be made aware of how it works, perhaps with a special video describing it.

In economically depressed areas, it may take numerous bond attempts before one succeeds. It may be necessary for the school to combine with other nearby towns. You may have to try several different proposals.

Don't give up.

District Reorganization

Reorganization can cause major upheaval and serious community conflict. New faces on a combined school board or new administrators in the front office can be upsetting to voters.

The prospect of shutting one or more schools and merging student bodies can be disconcerting for students and parents alike. Cross-town rival schools or towns suddenly find themselves forced to cooperate after generations of academic, sports, and business competition.

If the school district has recently reorganized, this can be a bad time to seek funds for school improvement. It might be better to wait awhile for the dust to settle before proposing a school referendum.

If the school bond referendum involves building a large new school and closing several smaller schools, start early in laying groundwork of cooperation. Make sure each town or school is well represented on the committee. Open lines of communication between school districts or towns.

Host joint social events. Find opportunities where the separate entities can compete as one. Only after rivalry has softened and people see themselves cooperating will communities be able to work together.

Cost of the Bond

It would seem obvious that the smaller the dollar amount of a school bond, the higher percentage of approval. But generally the public will be more concerned with the reason than the amount. How will the money be spent? The proposed facility must be presented as functional, efficient, and a long-term solution to a great need.

The cost to the taxpayer is also very important. Many voters will not take the time to figure exactly how bond approval will affect taxes. They will only have the impression that it will lighten their wallets.

Describe the proposed increase in human, daily terms. Is it equivalent to the cost of a newspaper or a cup of coffee per day? If offered up in small sips, the school bond will not seem so difficult to swallow.

People must be made aware that bonded debt is necessary. Just as most people must take out a mortgage to buy a house or a loan to buy a car, a city or town must borrow money to build the big-ticket items that benefit everyone. No bonded indebtedness, no progress.

ODDS AND ENDS

Below is a recap of the factors that lead to the best chance of a successful bond election:

- The school district has not recently reorganized.
- There is relatively low private school enrollment in the district.
- The district population is on the rise.
- The district has a healthy, diverse tax base.
- The district property tax levy is low.
- Voter turnout is low.

This last point may seem surprising, but it's true. If school bond supporters are quietly motivated and the opposition is not riled, a bond proposal is more likely to be approved. If the referendum fails on the first try, higher turnout on the next attempt is more likely to succeed—*if* you do a good job of educating and motivating the voters.

Hardly ever are all these ducks lined up at once. Take a close look at the special interests that make up your community and gauge your school situation carefully. If you feel the time is right for a school bond attempt, go for it.

> *What greater or better gift can we offer the republic than to teach and instruct our youth?*
>
> Cicero, Roman statesman

9

Opposing Views

There will be opposition to every proposed change in every community, everywhere. Count on it.

Any community can easily come up with at least 50 reasons to reject a school bond issue. As the German dramatist Friedrich Hebbel put it, "There are people who always find a hair in their soup for the simple reason that when they sit down before it, they shake their heads until one falls in."

The "no" reasons may be general, ill-formed, or not directly related to school improvement. The more common ones are found in . . .

THE SEVEN STEPS TO STAGNATION

1. We've never done it that way.
2. We're not ready for that yet.
3. We're doing OK without it.
4. We tried it that way once, and it didn't work out.
5. It costs too much.
6. That's not our responsibility.
7. It won't work.

It is the committee's job to eliminate as many "no" reasons as you can with soft words and hard information.

THE OPPONENTS

In school bond initiatives, opposition comes in two basic types—the honest and the ugly.

Honest opponents are sensible members of the community who, for a variety of reasons, oppose the school bond. Their reasons may be valid or dumb, but the honest opponents at least are straightforward.

They may think the school proposal is too grandiose. They might consider the site too far for their children to walk. They may believe they cannot afford the added tax burden, no matter how necessary school improvement might be.

They may or may not be open to a change of heart. They are usually willing to debate the issues in an up-front, although sometimes rancorous, manner.

Honest opponents should be encouraged to express their opinions. This is how disagreements are resolved.

Ugly opponents, on the other hand, have their minds made up, and nothing will change them. They will take a more personal approach to defeating the school bond. They are not above using less than honorable means to get their way.

The committee must understand the difference between these two types of opponents. How you deal with each can influence the outcome of the school bond venture. Your response to the opposition can also affect the emotional health of the community long after the school bond effort is over.

An argument is discourse between parties with different points of view. It should never be confused with fighting. Rather than become upset by it, you should welcome argument as an opportunity to make your case for bond levy passage.

If arguments produce more light than heat, they are very valuable tools. If an argument becomes overheated, however, the light of reason (and your chance at persuasion) will melt away.

Never wade into an argument head on. If you try to sail directly into the wind, you get nowhere. Search for common ground, then gently turn the argument to your point of view. By tacking in the general direction you want to go, you will make progress toward your goal.

COMMON ARGUMENTS AND HOW TO RESPOND TO THEM

"Taxes are too high already. We simply can't afford improvement."

Yes, taxes are a terrible burden. But we cannot afford to do nothing, either. The problems will not go away. Further delay will only lead to higher costs later.

The old school is expensive to run and maintain. A great deal of money would be needed to bring the old building up to current health, safety, and accessibility standards. Is this wise use of our limited resources?

The current school is overcrowded, and the facilities are not providing the kids with the space they need. Increased enrollment means increased tax base. A school bond will raise taxes little if at all.

Here is our opportunity to control our own taxes. You will see the benefit of this investment directly in your own community. Local tax, local results.

The sooner we get started, the sooner it will be built and paid for.

"The tax increase for a new school will drive us out of business. We need more business in town before we can afford a new school."

This is a chicken-and-egg situation. Surveys tell us one of the top concerns of businesses that plan to relocate is the quality and condition of the local schools. How much potential growth and top-quality employees have already gone elsewhere or were discouraged from settling here because of the poor condition of our schools?

If our schools remain in bad shape, we'll lose families to towns with more attractive schools. We need a new school to entice more business.

If you outgrow your business site, you move into larger more modern quarters. You improve air conditioning and lighting to make your customers more comfortable. Can we do less for the children in our community? They spend much more time each day in school than a customer does in any given business. How can we expect them to work in outdated, crowded, or unsafe conditions?

Investing in our children's education is one of the best investments we can make in our economic future. If the community invests in its future, it can count on having one.

"'They' should have taken care of the old buildings. If we give them more money, they'll just waste it. Let's not throw good money after bad."

Past maintenance and repair issues are outside the scope of this committee's efforts. By improving/expanding/building a new school, we will save money on extensive repairs and retrofitting to meet health and safety standards.

This bond will build (expand or upgrade) a new school and nothing else. No money goes to routine maintenance, increased salaries, or the sports program.

Let's not take out our frustration over past mistakes on the children. We must look forward.

"A little patch job will make that old building as good as new. It was good enough for me, and it's good enough for today's kids. Why, I walked nine miles to school through hip-deep snow . . ."

Chances are, the champion of this argument has not been inside the school for a long time. Organize an open house and a tour of the school facilities to demonstrate the need for improvement. Highlight the problems of the old school buildings in your audiovisual presentation.

Gather from the school superintendent copies of all engineering reports and building inspections describing the shortcomings of the school.

Be ready to compare the costs of facility repair versus replacement. Include the cost of maintenance, utilities, and upcoming requirements, such as handicapped accessibility.

Just as cars have become more comfortable and efficient, and houses are no longer lit with kerosene lamps, education and teaching methods have changed dramatically in the past few decades. There is so much more to learn, including mastering the learning tools (computers, the Internet, etc.).

Schools must keep up with the times to give our kids a competitive edge in the 21st century. The United States is way down the list of how much developed countries spend for education. This could put us and our kids at a disadvantage in competing for jobs and in world trade.

Many people feel competitive with other cities and towns in the region. Showcase school projects in other districts. Point out the advantages this has brought to those communities and how it might do the same for yours.

"We need to concentrate on education first. It's not the building but what goes on inside it that's important. Those teachers just aren't doing their jobs."

The teachers' classroom performance is outside the scope of this committee's work.

But if we wish to attract top-notch teachers and keep the excellent ones we have, we must have attractive facilities. We must provide an up-to-date, safe, well-designed school so teachers can teach more efficiently to today's standards.

Research has shown that, all else being equal, students in a modern, clean, uncrowded school do better academically than those in a substandard facility.

"The proposed school design is gold-plated, a monument to those egotistical school board members."

The school board's performance is outside the scope of the committee's work.

Be prepared to justify every aspect of the school design with sound logic. Emphasize the long-term nature of the school. Provide enrollment growth projections to justify a larger facility. If something seems too grandiose, or if you perceive strong opposition to a given part, consider dropping it or scaling back a bit. But never retreat from sound, basic design.

"We raised our kids, you raise your kids. My children are grown. I'm not paying any more taxes for schools."

In the past the entire community invested in the best schools of their day— the schools we now use. They understood that to become competent, taxpaying citizens, young people must be well educated.

Everyone benefits from modern education. Educating children is sound social insurance. The only means to maintain a democracy is through good public education. President Lyndon B. Johnson said, "Nothing matters more to the future of our country than education . . . for freedom is fragile if citizens are ignorant."

Unless one is prepared to be totally self-sufficient (do one's own dentistry, repair one's own car, mix one's own prescription drugs), one must depend on others. Let's ensure those others are as well prepared scholastically as they can be.

Are our young people missing out on scholarships or being turned away from top universities because of an outdated, inadequate learning environment?

Today we ask our kids for more respect. Yet if we do not provide adequate schools, we send them the message that we do not value them or their education. The kids are watching us and listening to us. What message are we sending them?

Poorly educated people can be expensive to society. We must support the students needs today so, as working citizens, they can support our needs tomorrow.

Many opponents have no direct contact with the school system. Many opposing arguments will have nothing to do with children.

During the information and education phases, the committee must identify as many of the specific "no" reasons as you can and try your best to resolve them.

Some "no" arguments may be valid. Be open to constructive criticism and alternate plans or designs. Be prepared to compromise without surrendering basic long-term goals. One who insists on having one's way in everything may end up with nothing at all.

As liaison between the school board and administration and the public, the committee will carry the public's complaints, suggestions, and worries to the board. The board must attempt to enlighten the people on the true facts and work to correct problems over which it has control. School district leaders must also listen carefully to what the public has to say.

During the education phase the committee will work hard to convince opponents to change their minds in favor of some form of improvement. You will do this through thoughtful, well-reasoned, civilized debate at focus group meetings and in newspaper columns, newsletters, and so on (see chapter 5, Publicity, and chapter 7, Ambassadors Club).

If you cannot change opponents' minds, fine. They are still sensible people of good will. They are opponents, not enemies. You simply disagree.

DO YOUR HOMEWORK

For every change or improvement proposed in your community, you will discover many of the same supporters and opponents raising the same arguments. If you can identify prominent members of each faction, you will save much energy and avoid many mistakes (see chapter 4, Research).

Research past school bond efforts early and well. Learn who were the prominent opponents and what actions they took. This will help you anticipate and respond to each opposing move.

Start by interviewing veterans of previous school bond attempts. Ask them who were the chief opponents. What was their beef? What did they do during previous campaigns? When did they begin?

Visit the newspaper archives covering previous school bond attempts. Study the articles, paid ads, and letters to the editor. What was the tone of the public debate? Was it reasonable and aboveboard? Did it become heated, rude, or personal?

Identify past campaign issues and their spokesmen. Which were the most important ones? Is the school situation the same now as then? Has anything changed?

Did opponents form their own "taxpayers' union" or "concerned citizens" group? Was their approach well researched and civilized or emotional and mean-spirited?

Early in the school bond effort, visit informally with identified major opponents. Ask them individually what they believed was wrong with past proposals. How would they have done things differently? Sometimes just including them in a meaningful dialogue can soften their resistance.

Invite them to your committee meetings to hash out differences. They probably won't come, but make them feel welcome anyway.

Keep in mind, though, if you have not convinced an opponent to support the school referendum by the end of the education phase, you can count on him to continue to oppose the bond. If you continue to chase him, you will drive his "no" vote into the ballot box.

Below are a few of the negative groups you may encounter:

THE COFFEE CLUB

This "club" may include a small group of retirees or merchants who meet over coffee at the café downtown or hang out together at a small local business.

They may or may not fall into the ugly camp, but often they are naysayers. In smaller communities this group can seriously undermine your campaign.

They are unlikely to come to the committee directly with questions or complaints, but it behooves you to find out what is bothering them.

Try hard to find a supporter who is part of the club and who feels comfortable sitting in with them. This supporter will keep track of the coffee crowd's complaints and the rumors they may pass around. "Spy" is too strong a title for this supporter because he will make no secret of his opinion of school support. He will carry information in both directions. His opinion will carry more weight with his fellow club members than any arguments the committee can muster.

If you decide the coffee club is hopelessly closed minded and mean, make no further attempt to contact them. Outwardly ignore them, but pay close attention to what they say. Challenge any and all misinformation they generate, but never directly confront the people who spread it. This will only rile them and energize their rumor mill.

THE TAX HATERS

Resistance to all taxes is a primal instinct with some people. People are most interested in that which directly affects them. If all they have to think about is the tax increase, that is a strike against the bond levy. Never underestimate the tax issue regarding school improvement.

Be open and unapologetic about the tax increase. Be ready with the facts. Compare your town's taxes with other cities and towns in your area. Remind people that there will be concrete, positive results from the tax increase, benefits they will see every day.

The amount of the bond asking is very important to this group. Their rule of thumb is "less is better." Make them aware that there is no fat in the bond proposal and that there is great need for improvement.

Don't push these people too hard. Pressure may rouse them to organize.

ORGANIZED OPPOSITION

Never underestimate or ignore opponents. If you fail to identify and acknowledge opposing views, those who hold them can quickly unite into opposition groups. These groups can be very damaging to a school bond effort.

Organized opponents might include a local taxpayers' union, ethnic or religious groups, or private school supporters.

If a group has already formed, it is generally a waste of time to try to convince them to support a school bond. At worst, the committee's overtures may spur them to stronger effort to defeat the bond.

Instead, the committee must work hard to deny these groups solid reasons on which to hang their campaign. Don't try to fight the direction and speed of the opposition's course. Take the wind out of their sails with soft smiles, a winning attitude, and cold, hard facts.

Where opposition is strongly entrenched in the community, it can create a monolithic roadblock to all progress. In this case, you must go around it by publicly ignoring it and taking your case directly to the people.

Opponents will be ever vigilant for weakness: a divided or reluctant school board, an unpopular school board member or superintendent, a political leader who opposes school improvement, public apathy or ignorance of the issues, or racial or religious conflict.

The committee's best approach to opposition is to counter arguments with facts in an indirect, non-confrontational manner. Never dwell on the negative. Always concentrate on the future and the needs of the children. Opponents seldom wish to be portrayed as ogres and scrooges. It is harder for them to say "no" to the community's children and their legitimate needs.

By focusing on the shortcomings of the school facilities and how those problems can be solved, the committee stays on the high road.

THE BAD GUYS

Then there are the other opponents, the ugly opposition. These bad guys are usually fewer in number than you'd think, but they have big mouths and they do vote.

Their strength lies in the fondness of many people to listen to conspiracy theories and vicious gossip, even if deep down the listener knows the information is suspect. As Mark Twain said, "A lie can travel halfway around the world while the truth is putting on its shoes."

Unlike forthright opposition, the "uglies" can represent the dark side of a school bond—or any political campaign. They are less than honorable opponents who attack through smear tactics, rumors, and misinformation.

Some uglies may oppose all taxes and will do anything they can to prevent an increase. Others may have a hidden agenda: a personal grudge against a school board member, suspicion of anything new, or nostalgia for the "good old days."

The stronger the uglies, the poorer your chance of success. Worse, if the committee handles the uglies poorly, quarrels and grudges can boil up that will last for years. These rifts can make the community a less pleasant place to live. They can also lessen the chances for success of future bond initiatives.

Unorganized, these are the naysayers who bad-mouth the bond proposal and the committee in the coffee shop, in the workplace, at the antique club, and on the op-ed page of the newspaper.

When the bad guys organize, as a committee of "concerned taxpayers" or "citizens against waste," they can present a formidable problem. By hiding behind the banner of preventing waste, they try to stop all progress in the community.

If you're lucky, the uglies will not pop up at all. Every town has its share of grouches. If they are few or don't have much clout, you can simply ignore them. If the community has a knot of mean-spirited grumps who can command the attention of a large number of people, you have a problem that must not be overlooked.

Generally the uglies will avoid face-to-face contact with the committee, but they will say the most outrageous things behind your back. They may attack the integrity and motivations of committee members, the school board, and bond supporters in general. They may personalize the issues and try to derail the school bond with rumors, slander, innuendo, insults, and side issues.

In an attempt to frighten business people from supporting the school bond, the uglies may threaten to organize a boycott of supporting businesses. At worst and very rarely, they may resort to personal threats, physical attacks, and vandalism.

HOW TO DEAL WITH THE UGLIES

The committee can strengthen or weaken the uglies to some degree. Your guiding light should be the knowledge that most people are reasonable and of good will. Most folks have an innate sense of fairness and will not be taken in by unsupported rumors.

Also, most people want to be associated with winners. If the voters feel the bond issue is going to pass on election day, they are much more likely to ignore the doom-and-gloom crowd and vote "yes." It's up to the committee to show unwavering confidence and a positive attitude.

Your best approach to the uglies is to treat them like everyone else: in a direct, friendly, open manner.

Consider adopting the marshmallow as the committee mascot. The *marshmallow?* Sure. It's hard to punch a marshmallow. It's soft and springy. It bounces right back as sweet as before. As ancient philosopher, Aleyn, said, "The true and noble way to kill a foe is not to kill him. You, with kindness, may so change him that he shall cease to be a foe, and then he is slain."

As Oscar Wilde said, "Always forgive your enemies—nothing annoys them so much"—or disarms them. Smile at ugly frowns. Respond to meanness with gentle courtesy.

It will be harder to be cool and patient with this bunch because they will try hard to push the committee off course. Slander is a classic tactic to embroil you in mean and meaningless side issues.

Simply ignore the ugly personal stuff. But when you detect misinformation concerning the bond issue, your response must be swift and unemotional. Respond only to the issue. Direct your response to the public at large, never to individuals.

Remember, you have the high ground. You represent the children and community improvement. Never sink to the uglies' level. If you lose your temper or respond to them in kind, you will be truly lost and so will be your campaign.

Vent your frustration among yourselves. Write down nasty responses in the most horrible language you can think of. Then collect all that anger and plots of revenge, put them in a big envelope, and set fire to it (not under an ugly's porch, please!).

Avoid giving the uglies any opportunity to vent in public. Avoid any direct contact with them. Never debate them in front of large audiences. You will be obliged to play fair. They won't.

Keep your focus group meetings small. Although the occasional heckler may disrupt an occasional meeting, the uglies usually are not motivated to go around and upset every one.

If you do encounter a noisy ugly during a focus group meeting, keep a cool head stuffed with hard facts. And leave your emotions at home (see chapter 7, Ambassadors Club).

RESPONDING TO THE UGLIES

Some sound arguments may be phrased in ugly ways. Do not ignore these arguments. If they are valid, they must be addressed. Here are a few examples of wrong and right ways to respond:

Attack: The committee is hiding the fact that hooking the school up to city utilities will cost the taxpayers an extra quarter of a million dollars . . .

Wrong: This committee is hiding nothing from the electorate. We are trying hard to be honest with this community, unlike some other groups we know!

Right: Utility hookups are included in the bond asking. There will be no additional cost to the district.

Attack: This new school would be located so far out of town that our children will get lost or freeze to death before they can get there.

Wrong: What nonsense! Nobody's going to freeze or lose his way . . .

Right: After thorough study by interested citizens, the school board, the committee, and the architect, the proposed site for the new school was deemed the best choice. It is the closest, most centralized site with adequate space for a new school. It is in the path of the city's future growth . . .

Attack: As soon as we pass this bond, the money will be diverted to higher teachers' salaries (perks for the school board, new football uniforms) . . .

Wrong: Everybody knows the teachers deserve higher pay. That new district minivan can be easily justified . . .

Right: School bond money can be used only for construction (renovation, addition) specified in the bond asking. No bond funds can be used for operating expenses, salaries, or routine maintenance.

The uglies may try to pull the committee off course through side issues. Do not be distracted and respond to arguments outside of the scope of the school bond. If they are bond-related, turn these arguments to your advantage.

Attack: The proposed school will be a new palace, a monument for that incompetent principal . . .

Wrong: The question of the principal's competence is a thorny one over which our committee is divided . . .

Right: The proposed school will be a no-frills, modern facility. The efficient design will help the students achieve . . .

Attack: Once they get this school built, the next thing they'll want to build is a new performing arts theater. One thing will lead to another, and we'll all be on our way to the poorhouse.

Wrong: According to our survey results, the committee finds strong support for a new theater . . .

Right: A performing arts theater is not included in the bond asking. The question of a theater is outside of the scope of this committee's work.

Attack: The committee is made up of a bunch of transients bent on raising our taxes then moving away.

Wrong: It ain't so, Joe, and this is why . . .

Right: No response.

The uglies may start rumors that community leaders who support the referendum are actually opposed to it.

Be on the lookout for photo opportunities that bring together prominent supporters, school board members, and other elected officials in committee-sponsored events. Ask supporting opinion leaders to put their endorsements *in writing*. Ask them to endorse the school bond publicly on radio or TV, in newspaper ads, or in an interview for the newsletter (see chapter 5, Publicity, and chapter 11, The Campaign).

THE POISON PEN

A tactic sometimes employed by the uglies is the poison pen letter. This letter is mailed, hand-delivered, or published in the newspaper right before election day. It is the bad guys' attempt to get in the last word. It may or may not be signed, or the authors may hide behind a bogus committee name such as "Citizens Against Waste."

This letter can contain anything the uglies' dark little hearts can dredge up: untruths about the bond and slanderous attacks on the committee members, the school board, teachers—you name it.

If the uglies have used this tactic in previous campaigns, members of the research subcommittee will have forewarned the committee.

What to do?

Don't lose your heads! Study the letter carefully and make a list of its major points. Ask yourselves, have you thoroughly and accurately covered all the issues in the final newspaper, newsletter, and broadcast ads? Yes? Is there any important relevant issue in the letter that might affect the outcome of the election? No? Then there is no need to respond.

If you believe that serious damage might have been done by this last-minute attack, write a well-reasoned, issue-oriented, unemotional response. It must address only those points directly related to the bond. It will refute inaccuracies and clear up confusion. Of course, you will not respond in any way to personal attacks!

Reactivate the canvassers and have them hand-deliver your response letter door to door (see chapter 12, The Canvass).

Remember, reasonable citizens—and most people are—will see through the poison pen letter. Most will not be swayed by it. Many will be offended.

LAST-MINUTE MEDIA BLITZ

Does your research show that opponents to previous school bonds flooded the media with last-minute radio and TV ads, letters to the editor, and paid ads from "concerned taxpayers" associations?

Prepare to overwhelm and bury this last-ditch effort with a positive media blitz of your own. By examining the newspapers during past campaigns, you'll be ready for whatever may be coming.

Time your response to appear at the same time or, if possible, after the opposition's big push (see chapter 11, The Campaign).

MARSHMALLOW PHILOSOPHY

Remember the 25/50/25 ratio (see chapter 4, Research)? No matter how hard you try, roughly 25 percent of the people will oppose the school bond. They may have valid reasons, stupid reasons, or no reason at all. An old Somali saying holds that, "It is impossible to awaken a person who is pretending to be asleep."

At the end of the education phase, stop trying to bring them around to your point of view. If you push the negative 25 percent too hard, you will only succeed in hardening their resolve and galvanizing them to action.

Instead, during the campaign phase, shift your efforts to identifying supporters and ensuring that their "yes" votes get into the ballot box.

Opposition will show a different face in each community. You can place the committee way ahead of the opposition by thoroughly researching past campaigns. Then you will understand the opposition and be prepared to deal with it effectively.

Keep your head and hold your temper at all cost. Never burn the opposition's yard signs. Never shout or wave your arms around. If you are personally insulted, do not respond at all.

Most people have an innate sense of fairness. They will be appalled and embarrassed by ugly tactics. They will respect the committee for restraint and grace under fire.

The best way for the committee to avoid stirring up turmoil that will outlast the campaign is to present a cordial, open face to supporter and opponent alike. Provide accurate information in a calm, courteous manner. Remember the marshmallow.

Stay focused on your goal—school improvement and the kids.

Finally, never lose track of the big picture. Remember from the very first to the very last day of a school bond effort, life will go on after election day. Try hard to avoid turning opponents into lifelong enemies. Supporters and opponents alike are your friends, neighbors, colleagues, and customers. You will all have to live, work, and play together after the school bond question has been decided.

10

Fund Raising

The school improvement committee is made up of all volunteers. So you don't need any money, right?

Sadly, as much as you are willing to give in time and effort, certain items and activities will require the "long green." Advertising, printing, premiums, the audiovisual presentation, postage, and paper—all cost money.

How much money is enough, you ask? The answer is, "As much as you have." You can achieve great things on a shoestring budget. You'll need lots of hard-working volunteers, a dollop of talent, and plenty of imagination. But the more money you have to spend, the more you can do.

How do you raise it, store it, keep track of it, and report it?

The first section of this chapter (the fun part) will cover how to raise funds. The second part contains nuts and bolts for the treasurer.

TIME FOR STUPID IDEAS

Call a serious meeting of all committee members. Sequester yourselves. Carefully and calmly consider various options to raise funds.

No! No!! No!!!

Come to this meeting in a funny hat. Stand up, walk around. Play silly music, dance, and sing songs. Loosen up. The aim of this meeting is to come up with the most absurd, stupid, and wacky ideas you can imagine. Work yourselves into a brainstorm.

"Let's invite the students to march in a tin pan parade down Main Street. The kids will use trash can and sauce pan lids as cymbals. One kid will pass the tin pan as a collection plate."

"Let's sell erasers door to door to 'Erase our school's problems.'"

"Let's soak the school board members in a dunking booth. Three tries for a dollar."

"Let's hold an 'Ugliest Classroom Contest,' $1 per vote."

"Let's win prize money by entering a float in the 4th of July parade."

"Let's throw a dance in honor of the teacher of the year."

"Let's have a bake sale and sell 'Food for Thought' or 'Brain Food.'"

"Why, to get a new school for this town, let's take off our clothes and fly down Main Street."

Get the idea? Write down these "dumb" ideas on paper airplanes and fly them around. Let yourselves go. Have fun!

Of course, you will throw out some weird schemes. Others will be toned down, combined, or changed into something else. But, believe it or not, most of these goofy ideas have been used successfully as actual committee fund raising activities.

No doubt your school improvement effort will last long enough to run through some big community celebration such as a fall festival or the county fair. These are perfect opportunities to raise money and community awareness at the same time.

One word of caution: remember, the image you present to the public ultimately will be used by the voters to judge the bond. Always conduct these events in a positive, open, and lighthearted fashion. Get too serious and you will lose them. Never use these activities to embarrass, annoy, or condemn opponents. This will damage your public image and activate enemies.

If you involve children in an event, be sure they understand and truly support the school improvement effort. And always obtain their parents' consent.

SERIOUS MONEY

You can't be silly all of the time. You're going to have to find some serious money for your campaign. Where should you look?

Seed money will probably come from simply passing the hat among committee members. This should get you started.

During the earliest, or information, phase, it is not appropriate to ask people for money. Remember, this first phase is simply for fact finding. You are exploring citizens' views on the school situation. This is the time to enlist supporters and volunteers, not to seek contributions.

If you decide after the information phase that there is enough support out there to try for a school bond, the need for money will begin in earnest. As the ambassadors start conducting focus group meetings during the education phase, you can start passing the hat at those meetings.

Who else are you going to tap?

- *Parent-teacher organizations:* Parents with children in the affected schools will be your biggest supporters. Parent-teacher organizations are usually experienced in raising funds. If they can't or won't help you directly, they should be able to give you some good fund raising ideas.
- *Teacher's unions, both local and state*: They have a direct and active stake in decent school facilities. They may be eager to make a donation to the committee. Check with the local union representative. He can give you the names and numbers of the state leadership.
- *Community service organizations*: Rotary, Lions, Optimists, Elks, American Legion . . . Many of these groups focus on the well-being of children. They know that good schools are good for the community.
- *The business community*: Call on local business people either door-to-door or through the chamber of commerce. Most are aware that good schools are good for business.
- *Local churches*: Visit with the local clergy. They can ask their congregations for support on your behalf. They can pass along your request to their various auxiliary groups. These groups may offer to raise funds for you. Also this is fertile ground for volunteers.
- *Philanthropic organizations*: Is there one or several in your region? These groups may offer matching grants—a nifty way to double your money. Don't be bashful about approaching them for help. The worst that can happen is you will come away empty-handed.
- *Private donors*: Check your research. Who supported bond efforts in the past? Chances are they will be willing to help out again.
- *State funds*: Are grants available for school improvement? Are state lottery funds earmarked for education? Check with your state department of education. Be careful. Public funds cannot be used for campaign purposes.

Always read the fine print. Donations and contributions may come with strings attached. Be sure you can live with the conditions.

Don't be shy. Passing the hat for the committee is not begging. The money raised will be used for the community's benefit. Also, don't take it personally if you are turned down. There are many good reasons why people will not donate.

Every committee member should keep a sharp eye out for fund raising opportunities. There is usually more money around than you would think. You just have to hunt to find it.

PUBLIC VS. PRIVATE FUNDS

Can public money be used in a school bond campaign? In general, public funds such as school district, city, or county money can be used for information and educational purposes only. For example, tax money can be used to inform the public of shortcomings in the schools and to produce estimates on how much money will be required to repair or replace school facilities (printed brochures and pamphlets). Public money can be used to print announcements or buy ad space or time in newspaper, radio, and TV for upcoming meetings concerning school issues. It can be used to pay for printed posters and notices of when and where the election will be held.

Public money cannot be used to persuade people to vote in favor of the school bond. The school board, city council, or county commissioners cannot spend money from the public coffers to campaign for the bond measure.

School bond opponents will be quick to squawk if they think tax money is in any way promoting the school bond. It is best to use as much private funding as possible to avoid controversy—even on activities where it is technically legal to use public money.

A citizens' committee has much more leeway than public agencies to raise and spend funds. The committee is free to say and do practically anything it feels will advance school bond approval.

FUND RAISING AND THE LAW

Now for the nuts and bolts . . .

It is the treasurer's responsibility to learn the rules covering campaign finance. Each state will have different regulations on what can and cannot be done with campaign funds. These regulations change from time to time, so it is important to seek out the latest information when setting up the bookkeeping. Contact your state's office of the secretary of state or office of the county clerk. Each state will have an election handbook.

Check the filing schedule. You may have to file campaign finance reports more than once during the campaign. Your reports must be timely, complete, and accurate. Check the regulations on the types of fund raising activities and expenditures that are allowed and the limits on the amount of anonymous contributions you can collect.

There may be exceptions depending on the amount of money you raise. Even if you start down the road to a school bond and raise funds and then disband the committee, you may still be required to file a report.

Latch on to a local attorney with political campaign knowledge, preferably someone who has run for office and has experience in filing campaign reports with the state. You'll need someone—preferably one who will help out *pro bono* (free)—who can keep you on the right side of campaign finance laws.

The treasurer will open a bank account for the committee. This account must be kept separate from all other funds.

Contributions

A contribution is made for a political purpose if it is intended to influence an election or a question submitted to the voters. Reportable contributions include gifts, subscriptions, in-kind contributions, pledges, leans, advances or deposits of money, or any other thing of value.

- Keep a list of the name and street address of every contributor, no matter how small the donation. Accept no anonymous contributions. If a cash-filled envelope is slipped under your door marked only with the committee's name, turn it over to a tax-exempt charity. Sorry. Unidentifiable cash contributions (such as passing the hat at a barbecue or committee-sponsored event) may be kept up to a certain amount. Contributions exceeding that amount must be donated to a tax-exempt organization.
- Non-cash contributions, such as donated radio or newspaper advertising, must be reported as a contribution in-kind. List each contribution in the amount it would have cost had it been paid for. This does not include free column space, news releases, or public service announcements.
- Pledges should be posted at the time they are made, the same as cash or in-kind contributions.

Expenditures

Expenditures include payment or promise to pay and transfer or distribution of money or anything of value. Any debts, both paid or forgiven, must be itemized and reported.

- Pay all expenses by check from the committee's account. If you must use petty cash, establish a formal fund and keep careful record of the amount, date, and purpose of each payment. Just to be on the safe side, you might want co-signing authority for at least two committee members.
- Keep an accurate log of the full name and street address of who was paid for what. List the name and address of those who actually provided the goods or services if it is different from those who received payment.
- An expenditure is anything of monetary value. This includes in-kind donations. In-kind donations must be reported as both contributions and expenditures.

BOOKKEEPING AND REPORTING

Be sure to file reports when required. Figures must be brought forward from one report to the next if you must file more than one report. And don't forget the final campaign report after the election. The final report is filed after all political activity has stopped, all debts have been retired, and the campaign bank account has been closed. You may have to file special information on people or organizations that contributed more than a certain amount.

Sounds pretty scary and official, but don't be afraid. Election fiscal rules are not meant to discourage you, just to keep the campaign aboveboard. Some states provide reporting software you can run on a personal computer and allow you to file your reports electronically.

And don't worry about where the money will come from. It's out there. You just have to be creative in rounding it up. There will be no problem in finding ways to spend it, especially during the campaign.

11

The Campaign

This is the home stretch, so give it all you've got. You've reached the campaign phase. Now is the time to kick into high gear and to pull everything together for the final push.

Where do you stand on the eve of the school bond campaign?

No doubt you feel you have now met every person in town. You have made many friends and probably a few enemies. You have finished the information phase, which opened a conversation among the committee, the school board, and the public. You have gathered information on what the community and the school board believes is needed. You have thoroughly researched past school bond efforts, both successful and unsuccessful. You have uncovered the leaders of the opposition and have become familiar with their arguments.

The education phase is over. You have hosted school tours, paraded floats, made speeches, and sold brain food. Most people are now aware of the shortcomings of the old school. You have explored all the issues and informed the community of the various needs and options for school improvement. You have examined and presented the pros and cons of possible solutions.

The ambassadors have shown the video or slide show to one and all. You have built a bridge between the community and the school board. The committee's newspaper columns, newsletters, articles, and press releases have reached everyone who would read, look, or listen.

Through your research into past school bond attempts, you are prepared to counter the arguments and moves of the opposition.

Most important, you've slowly and steadily compiled a master list of all the supporters you could find, those both registered and not registered to vote.

Ideally, with the public's input through the committee, the school board has settled on a suitable plan. The board has announced the bond referendum and scheduled election day.

Thus begins the campaign phase. The time has come to sell the plan the school board has adopted. *Your campaign task, pure and simple, is to motivate identified supporters to go to the polls and vote "yes."*

HOW LONG DOES THE CAMPAIGN LAST?

Although you have been planning and preparing for it for months, the campaign phase should last no longer than three to four weeks. If it lasts longer than that, you cannot keep up the pace or maintain voter interest. Besides, you don't want to give the opposition time to organize.

If your timing is right, the campaign tidal wave should crest on election day.

THE CAMPAIGN SLOGAN

If the committee hasn't already done so, choose a campaign slogan. This short phrase represents the razor-sharp distilled essence of the school improvement effort. It must be positive and forward-looking. Concentrate on the children. How will they benefit from a new school? Or concentrate on the community. How will the people benefit from a new school?

What will the slogan be? Sample slogans to hang a campaign on include:

- Education and Community—Growing Together
- Blue Ribbon Schools for Blue Ribbon Kids
- Kids, Community, Our Future
- A New School—Building for the Future
- Let's "Bond" Together for Our Children's Future
- For the Kids, for the Community
- Our Children's Future Is Now

Like the slogan, the tone of the campaign must be positive, enthusiastic, and confident of success. "This Tuesday our community will be taking a great step forward . . ." or "When the new school is built, we'll have achieved . . ." You get the idea.

If the committee publicly assumes the bond will pass, the voters will assume it will, too. Everyone wants to bet on the winning horse. Besides, a confident winning attitude discourages the opposition. "Why bother to vote? The school bond is going to pass anyway."

Conversely, each supporter must be convinced that his vote is vital to the success of the bond issue. He must believe that if he doesn't vote, the school bond will fail.

Repeat the slogan simply and often throughout the campaign. Include it on all campaign literature and state it on all radio and TV spots.

THE CAMPAIGN DIRECTOR

The campaign director is the person who coordinates all campaign activities. Although the campaign phase is relatively short, the director's job starts well before the final three to four weeks of the actual campaign.

He must be a real "people person" and a master of persuasion. He must be an efficient organizer. He must be able to prod his volunteers to do their best work without badgering them into mutiny. He must thrive on bedlam and love to do many things at once. He must be flexible and ready to tackle sudden and unforeseen crises. He must not be afraid of hard work and long hours. He must love to win.

How the campaign director organizes and distributes the workload depends on the size of the community and the number and talents of the help that is available. As with the committee, jobs should be tailored to talent, not the other way around. Committee members who are not working on other things should be prepared to pitch in on specific campaign tasks.

Campaign duties in larger school districts might be parceled out by precinct. Precinct captains will be responsible for the volunteers working within each precinct, and only the captains will report directly to the director. Smaller towns can organize less formally.

CAMPAIGN VOLUNTEERS

The campaign phase will need the help of many volunteers. How many? The more the merrier. Tasks spread out among many people mean less work for each individual.

Remember, too, *each volunteer is a "yes" vote.*

Start with your trusty master list of supporters. Other sources of volunteers are parents, teachers, school booster organizations, clergy and religious groups, business leaders, and members of civic organizations, hobby clubs, and cultural and sporting groups.

Don't forget students. They are energetic and enthusiastic. They may be directly affected by the outcome of the school bond election.

Ask volunteers to recruit others. In a grassroots campaign, "bring a friend" takes on a whole new meaning.

Don't be shy about tapping supporters to work on the campaign. Many people will be willing to help, but they won't take the initiative to volunteer. They will be happy to pitch in if you ask them in person. Don't just call people up and ask for their help with the campaign. When you contact a potential volunteer, have a specific job in mind. Describe the task and estimate the time needed to complete it.

Offer volunteers a menu of useful and meaningful tasks. Some people will be more enthusiastic about one job but hate the thought of doing another, so be ready to offer a choice of jobs.

If a potential volunteer says he'd like to help but hasn't got the time, be prepared to propose a job that can be done in small increments. Nearly everyone can find time in their busy schedules to address a few postcards or make a couple of phone calls.

For every assignment, make sure each volunteer gets detailed instructions, clear guidelines, and proper training. When volunteers contact the public directly, they represent the school(s), the school board, and the committee. People are very impressed when someone makes the effort to visit with them personally. If this contact is positive, it can benefit your cause enormously; however, misinformed or ill-prepared volunteers can undo months of hard work.

Set a definite deadline for each task. The person responsible for the volunteers' work must follow through and check on the work. Each volunteer must have the name and number of the responsible person for each job so problems can be resolved promptly.

CAMPAIGN ACTIVITIES

The key to getting your message across is to say the same thing in many different ways.

Below is a menu of campaign activities and how to use them. Don't feel you must do them all. Each community has a different way of going about things. Choose the ones you think would be most effective and for which you have the time, talent, energy, and volunteers.

THE BROCHURE

This is the campaign centerpiece. Your goal is to ensure each and every voter receives a brochure before election day. (See chapter 5, Publicity, for design and content. Sample text is shown in appendix D.)

The brochure will be distributed during the canvass if it is conducted door-to-door (see chapter 12, The Canvass).

In addition, or instead, volunteers can distribute brochures at shopping centers or other public places (not on school grounds or in public buildings). Make sure you have the blessing of the store owner if you set up outside his door. Leave stacks for distribution at supporting businesses and churches. Begin to distribute copies at focus group meetings as soon as the brochures become available.

MOBILIZING BUSINESS SUPPORTERS

For the past several months, the ambassadors have been making the rounds to businesses and chamber of commerce meetings. Now it is time to stir up business support.

Distribute campaign posters to all supporting businesses. Ask proprietors to display them prominently. Give business people extra campaign ribbons, buttons, pencils, and so on. Ask them to wear the campaign colors and distribute campaign tokens to customers.

Business people, especially in small towns, may be in favor of school improvement but reluctant to publicly back a school bond issue. They may fear stirring up controversy and losing the business of school bond opponents.

Be gentle but firmly persuasive in gaining their public support. Unless the town has a very wide mean streak, fears of retaliation are groundless. What's good for the community (an attractive school system) is good for business. What's good for the children is good for everyone.

TEACHER AND STAFF SUPPORT

Teachers are sometimes asked by the superintendent or school board to keep a low profile during school bond campaigns. The argument goes that teachers are the ones who will benefit most directly from a bond. They shouldn't be seen as asking the community "to build them a palace."

But the campaign will be diminished if the teachers and staff are not strongly involved. If the public gets the impression that teachers are not enthusiastic about the school bond, they will think the teachers don't care. Worse, the opposition might claim that, because the teachers have no opinion, they must believe the current school situation is fine. "If the teachers don't care, why should we?"

Besides, by discouraging the teachers from showing their support, you deny the campaign a large number of motivated volunteers and strong advocates. You can't have too many of those. Remember, every volunteer is also a "yes" vote.

Invite teachers and staff to distribute brochures, display yard signs, wear buttons and ribbons, and hang posters (never on school property or during schooltime).

Invite them to take part in the canvass. Ask them to write letters to the editor or take out paid ads in the local paper.

Recruit the school superintendent, administrators, and school board members to take part in the canvass. If they are willing, include them in roundtable or panel discussions on radio or TV.

But be careful. Encourage the school board members or superintendent to become involved in the campaign only if they are popular or widely respected. An unpopular or controversial school official can do the campaign more harm than good.

Strife between school district personnel and the community can lead to bickering over side issues. If the board, for example, is carrying too much political baggage, the committee should distance itself from board members during the campaign. Concentrate on school improvement, educational needs, and, of course, the children. Don't be dragged into personal and other side issues.

THE SIGNATURE POSTER

The signature poster is very effective in smaller towns, but it becomes unwieldy and impersonal in larger ones. It is sort of a cross between a roster of supporters and a petition. As citizens sign it, neighbors and friends can see who supports the bond. As the number of signatures grows, the poster becomes a graphic show of support for school improvement.

Circulate several large (two-by-three-foot) stiff-backed sheets of white paper. Attach a bold black marker with a string. On the top of each, write something like, "*We Support The (Date) Bond Issue for Improvement of Our*

School." Rotate one among the local supermarkets, one among the banks, another at the various discount stores, yet another among the schools in the district.

Take a signature poster to each focus group meeting during the campaign phase. Ask supporters to sign it after the ambassador's presentation.

Just before the election and before the last newspaper comes out, gather the posters and combine all the signatures onto one large page. Place this page as a giant ad in the final newspaper edition before election day.

ENDORSEMENTS

On every important issue, people look around to see how others feel about it. The opinions of community leaders carry an enormous amount of weight. There are several ways these people can help your campaign. They can offer to help conduct focus group meetings. During the campaign phase, they can make radio, TV, or print ads urging voters to support the school bond. Or they can simply express their support informally at work, at meetings, and at play. When they create a "buzz" in favor of school improvement, these opinion leaders can lure many others into the voting booth.

All committee members should keep a sharp eye out for prominent supporters during focus group meetings. Long before the campaign phase, begin collecting endorsements from the mayor; city, county, and state representatives; chamber of commerce officers; and prominent business, civic, and religious leaders. Encourage them to publicly express their support.

Photo opportunities are doubly good, instantly linking the supporters with the committee and your cause. This prevents the opposition from unknowingly (or otherwise) claiming opinion leaders.

The publicity manager will maintain the list of potential endorsements. For maximum impact, he will save the endorsements for the campaign phase. At that time he will ask these supporters to read a statement on the radio or write a letter to the editor or take out an ad in the newspaper.

If the school bond election coincides with municipal elections, try to get all the candidates to endorse the bond.

VOTER REGISTRATION

No matter how much you favor the school referendum, you cannot vote if you're not registered. This little detail can cost precious support.

Just before the deadline for voter registration, set up a special time and place for non-registered supporters to register (see the county registrar for details). Glean their names from the master list. Call each one to offer him this special opportunity.

CAMPAIGN TOKENS

These are small items people wear, display, or attach to their cars to show support for the bond measure. They turn supporters into roving advertisements. They also remind people to vote.

Campaign premiums might be door hangers, balloons, bookmarks, pencils, erasers, ribbons, buttons, pencils, giant paper clips, and refrigerator magnets. On these items can be printed your campaign slogan and whatever other information will fit. For ideas and prices, look through office supply catalogs used by businesses for advertising premiums or search the Internet under "campaign products."

Campaign ribbons can be custom-printed or made from a simple twist of ribbon in your campaign color attached to a safety pin. A button can be specially ordered or merely a paper cutout with your logo and slogan stamped or printed on it. Whatever you choose, make it easily identifiable with your campaign.

A length of ribbon in the campaign color attached to the car antenna makes an inexpensive, simple statement of support. These cheerful bits of ribbon give a little boost to all supporters.

Bumper stickers are expensive and hard to remove after the election. If you choose to print and distribute them, hand them out. Never stick them on cars, windows, or walls without permission.

When designing your tokens, include your logo, slogan, and the election date in the campaign color. Don't get too fancy or extravagant. Quantity is more important than quality. Slick tokens allow the opposition to ponder where all the money has come from. Remember, yours is a grassroots effort, not a gala production. Let your imagination be your guide.

Give yourself ample lead time. If you order tokens from commercial vendors, allow a comfortable margin for unforeseen problems and delays. If the tokens are to be handmade, start volunteers working on them well before they will be needed.

BILLBOARDS

They can be expensive, but they are worth it. Choose your locations well to receive maximum exposure, such as a busy intersection with traffic signals or adjacent to a popular store's parking lot. Reserve the locations well in advance, but plan to rent space for no longer than one month before the election. Keep the message bold and simple because the billboard will be viewed by busy people on the move. It never hurts to ask billboard owners to donate the space as a show of support.

YARD SIGNS

Yard signs are those smaller placards on sticks or wires stuck in the front yards of supporters and "sign jungles" of vacant corner lots. They can be homemade or professionally printed, depending on your funds or volunteer talent.

They should display the committee's logo, color, and slogan. A dark background with white or light lettering shows up best. Use a simple font and big, bold letters. The message must be very short and simple. Make the signs sturdy and weatherproof if possible. Ask all supporters to display them starting a couple weeks before the election. Vacant lots visible from busy intersections make excellent sign locations. Place them so motorists stopped for the traffic light can't help but notice them. Be sure to ask for the property owners' permission before installing them.

POSTERS

Posters are a quick visual reminder to get out and vote. They can be printed on fancy stock in several colors or copied on standard 8½-by-11-inch sheets of paper. (Your budget will be your guide.) Don't forget to use the campaign color. Include logo, slogan, and election date. Keep posters simple for quick recognition.

Ask private supporters and businesses to display posters in their windows. Have volunteers spread out and staple or tape them to every available pillar or post just before (within two days of) election day. Check with city officials first for rules of display.

PUBLIC EVENTS

How about staging a big campaign rally? Good idea?

Maybe, maybe not.

Before you plan one, carefully consider your campaign situation. Is there enough active community support to provide a good turnout? What if you invited the public to a rally and nobody came?

Gauge the strength and determination of the opposition. Are they noisy and unreasonable? Might they pack and disrupt the rally? A few rude, loud hecklers can wreak havoc and seriously damage your campaign.

As you plan public events, always focus on the children. What is all this hoopla about anyway? Kids, of course. They are the ones who suffer the outdated, crowded school conditions.

Consider children's concerts, street theater, a children's rally, or parade. Before involving children, though, be sure they really understand and support the event. Always get their parents' permission for them to participate.

THE MEDIA

For maximum impact, wait until the final week or ten days to launch your media blitz. The public's attention span is short. You don't want your campaign to peak too early. Build steadily toward the climax of election day. If your timing is right, the airwaves and the newspapers will be awash with your ads, news, letters, and campaign events during the last few days before the election.

Newspapers

If the local paper is a weekly, save your big push for the last newspaper before election day. Load that final edition with everything you've got. If it is a daily paper, spread everything out over the final week before election day.

Now is the time to activate endorsements by community opinion leaders. Their ads must stand out from the flood of commercial advertising that drenches us every day. Make the ads visually attractive and instantly recognizable. Every word must count. Graphics or pictures are more likely to catch the reader's eye. Photos including children are very effective. Try to include photos of prominent supporters in their endorsements.

Letters to the editor must fill the last two weekly newspaper editions or the final week's issues of the daily paper. Unless the opposition starts writing letters early, don't start yours too soon. You do not want to activate opposition letter writers to start a war of words on the op-ed page.

Don't assume supporters will write these letters by themselves. Throw a "letter to the editor" party. Ask people to bring a potluck dish and a letter supporting the school bond. If a supporter insists he is no good with words or suffers from writer's block, you can suggest topics, provide sample letters to work from, or even ghostwrite the letters. Have on hand a word processor or typewriter, writing materials, and stamped envelopes addressed to the newspaper editor. That way the letters will be finished, signed, and ready to send. The publicity manager will coordinate the distribution of these letters to cover all the newspapers in the district and will mail them at regular intervals.

Ideally the letters will cover every major issue and address and anticipate the main arguments of the opposition. Try to limit each letter to 100 to 150 words and to a single topic (see appendix C for samples).

Check with the newspaper for its requirements. *All letters must be signed and include a return address and telephone number. The newspaper will not print anonymous letters.*

Remind school board members to write a joint letter supporting the bond measure (see appendix B for sample). All board members must sign the letter. To ensure it will be published, ask them to buy advertising space in the paper and/or radio air time for it. They will have to take up a collection among themselves to pay for the ad. Personal ads purchased by the district superintendent and school principal(s) are also valuable.

The last newspaper before the election should be crammed with your pitch. Your research will have prepared you for all opponents' arguments. If the opposition mounts a last-minute push, the information you include in these final newspapers should anticipate, counter, and overwhelm it.

All print ads must show the name and street address of whoever paid for them. If the committee pays for the advertising, the name and home address of the treasurer is usually what is listed.

Television

Television spots are expensive, especially during prime time. There are many more effective ways to spend precious funds. If you do buy TV time, use it for maximum effect. Make every second count. Focus on the kids. Choose times and dates when supporters are most likely to see the ads.

Work to get as much free TV exposure as you can by taking part in roundtable discussions or interviews about the school bond. Beware that the format is helpful, not harmful, to your cause. Avoid hostile hosts or any setup that involves a direct confrontation with the opposition. You have little to gain and much to lose in such an arrangement.

Radio

Radio spots are usually much less expensive than you would expect. A 15- or 30-second spot repeated at different times of the day can be very effective in getting your message out. Radio is an effective place to use business endorsements.

Campaign ads broadcast on TV or radio must include the name of the purchaser. "Paid for by (Your) Committee, Money Baggs, treasurer" is all that is needed. The media will keep the street address on file and available for public review.

Look for free radio exposure through public service announcements. If possible, schedule committee members on local radio talk shows. Interviews are best with a question-and-answer format. As with television, avoid radio hosts who are biased against the referendum. Also avoid any arrangement that takes cold calls from listeners. This can set you up for direct, live confrontation with the opposition. A noisy loose cannon can do a lot of damage.

If you have a local talk show where call-in opinions are expressed, call in every day of the week before election day. Each day give a different reason why the town needs to vote "yes" for the school bond measure. Make these mini-spots short and concise.

Or assign a committee member or knowledgeable volunteer to listen to the show for the entire week before election day. This well-informed monitor should be prepared to quickly respond to misinformation and answer questions brought up by call-in participants.

Cable TV

Check with your local cable company. Does it have a bulletin board where announcements can be posted? Does it host a community issues forum?

Does the school district have a cable channel? It cannot be used to campaign for the referendum, but it can provide basic facts about the school situation and remind voters of election day.

Telephone

The telephone can be one of the most effective means of getting out the vote for a school bond measure. It requires a huge pool of volunteers to pull it off, but the results can spell the difference between success and failure.

A short phone call to supporters on the weekend before election day is a very effective reminder. Divide a copy of the master list of supporters among volunteers and call everyone on the list (see sample script in appendix D).

Open a telephone hot line the week or so before election day. Announce it in the column, in a newsletter, on the radio, and in TV ads. If phone volunteers can't answer a question right away, have them call a committee member immediately to track down an accurate response. Return the call as quickly as possible. Leave no question unanswered.

Computer

Communication through the Internet gains in importance every day. It is a great place to post all sorts of information to keep voters informed of the latest developments.

If you have a committee member who knows his way around cyberspace, have him create a simple web page devoted to information on the school referendum. If the committee has no computer expert, keep a sharp eye out for a supporter who can help you out. Or ask a local web designer to build you a web page. Advertise the web site and an e-mail address in all your campaign literature so net surfers can get information on the school bond measure. Ask the local Internet service provider to host your web site. If you have to pay, it is not very expensive and well worth the cost for a couple of months before the election.

Campaign Letter or Postcard

Sending a reminder letter to identified supporters also is a very effective way to get out the "yes" vote. It reminds people where and when to vote and briefly states why they should vote "yes" (see sample in appendix D).

It should be timed to arrive a day or two before the election.

The message should touch on the major campaign themes. It can help clear up final bits of misinformation. Its tone must be enthusiastic, positive, and confident. It must never address side issues or include responses to personal attacks.

For best effect:

- Use a good quality typewriter or printer.
- Include your logo or photos of children. Keep it simple and avoid busyness.
- At least one member of the committee should sign the letter.
- Personalize the letter or card in every possible way.
- Hand-written addresses receive more attention than typed or printed labels.
- To save time on envelope stuffing, fold the letter in thirds and address the back. Using a rubber stamp or self-stick address labels with the committee's name, address, logo, and phone number is a nice touch.

Check with the postmaster to see if you would benefit from the bulk mail rate. It could save you a lot of money.

Postcards are effective, and they are less expensive to mail. They have less space for detailed information but serve primarily to remind supporters to vote. Make every word count.

Send letters or postcards only to identified supporters who are registered to vote. The last thing you want to do is motivate opponents to "get out and vote."

If postage costs are beyond your means, reactivate canvassers to distribute the reminder letter or card on election eve (see chapter 12, The Canvass).

LAST-MINUTE PREPARATIONS FOR ELECTION DAY

By election eve the following activities should be organized and ready to go:

- A bank of several telephones and the volunteers to staff them for those last-minute calls to supporters to remind them to vote. This phone bank will serve as "Information Central" for the committee and the public on election day.
- Several volunteer drivers on call, ready to take people to the polls.
- A few baby-sitters standing by to watch children while their parents go to the polls.
- Poll watchers assigned to each polling place equipped with lists of registered voters.
- Runners ready to take voter information back to the phone bank (if poll watchers do not have access to phones).

GENERAL CAMPAIGN ADVICE

Consider each and every potential "yes" vote a precious gem. Don't pass up a single one. Assume that vote would be the one that wins (or loses) the day.

Never dwell on past events and mistakes. Avoid becoming involved in personality conflicts (an unpopular principal, squabbles over teaching styles). A common tactic of the opposition is to scatter your message with frivolous bickering. You are on the high road. Stay there.

Avoid side issues (crosswalks leading to the new school, reseeding the football field). They are little cuts that can bleed away your focus and energy.

Expect the unexpected. Research can help you avoid many surprises by seeing who did what, when, and how in past campaigns. Be prepared to respond swiftly, coolly, and accurately to last-minute problems.

Prepare well ahead of time. Be organized and disciplined. Stick to your plan. Follow through. Leave nothing to chance.

Thus, when the big day arrives, you'll be ready.

12

The Canvas

The winning margin of citizens may favor the bond issue, but the only way to win an election is to identify them and get their "yes" votes into the ballot box. Canvassing is one of the most efficient ways to accomplish this.

The canvass serves two purposes. First, it is a very effective method of locating supporters. Second, there is no better way to impress voters than to canvass them. You will run into a few cranks or mean-spirited opponents during a canvass. But you will find that most people appreciate the effort you make to contact them personally.

You can canvass by phone, but it is much more effective to go door to door. Personal contact is much more persuasive than a cold phone call. Plus a personal visit is the perfect opportunity to deliver campaign literature directly into the hands of potential voters.

If you conduct the canvass just before the voter registration deadline, it allows you time to get those unregistered supporters signed up.

The canvass should be conducted during the campaign and preferably before the deadline for voter registration. It should be done after the campaign brochure is completed so door-to-door canvassers can distribute the brochure while on their rounds.

As with the survey, the canvass should be conducted on a tight time limit. Why? Canvassing is a tedious, time-consuming task. It is best not to drag it out.

Also, the committee will need ample time to digest the information gathered in the canvass. Names of supporters will be transferred to the master list for contact before and/or on election day. Rides to the polls and baby-sitting services must be scheduled.

THE CANVASS COORDINATOR

It is time once again for the survey-canvass coordinator to swing into action. He will run the canvass much as he did the survey, although on a larger scale and a shorter time frame. After his long hiatus, he should be full of fresh ideas and energy. Good thing, too, because by now most of the committee members have been ground down to nubbins.

The canvass coordinator must be a firm taskmaster to make sure jobs are completed and deadlines are met. He must also be able to cajole and sweet-talk volunteers into quickly performing this difficult task.

This is also time for an infusion of lively, enthusiastic volunteers. The more canvassers you can put on the street, the smaller the area each will have to cover.

CANVASS PREPARATION AND TRAINING

Call a meeting of all volunteers who are willing to canvass: teachers, parents, high school students, business people, church leaders, and service club members. Ask school board members, administrators, and the superintendent to canvass, too. Enlist local politicians only if they are popular and are not currently running for office. This way you avoid partisan politicos with agendas of their own.

If the canvass is to be conducted door-to-door, divide the community as evenly as possible among all available volunteers. On a detailed city street map, assign each canvasser a specific area to cover. When possible, assign them to canvass their own neighborhoods. They will likely know the people better and feel more comfortable in their own territory.

If the canvass is to be done by phone, divide the local phone book pages equally among volunteer callers.

As with campaign volunteers in general, each canvasser represents the school district, the committee, and the school referendum. Make sure each volunteer is trained to properly and positively meet the public.

At the canvass meeting, thoroughly rehearse how canvassers are to contact people. Play acting is a great way to prepare canvassers for their task in what to say, what not to say, and how to avoid confrontations. Give them a hard time. Ask them tough questions. The more time they practice, the more prepared and confident they will be.

INSTRUCTIONS TO DOOR-TO-DOOR CANVASSERS

- Study the fact sheets and campaign literature so you are familiar with all the material. If anything is confusing, ask for clarification before you canvass.
- Suggested introduction: "Hello, my name is . . . I have volunteered to help distribute information about the upcoming school bond election. We hope you will take a few moments to read this literature. It contains information about the proposed school bond. May we count on your support on (election date)?"
- If the contact does not support the school bond, thank him politely and leave. If the respondent is unacquainted with the issue, give him a very short description of the proposal.
- If the respondent supports the bond, ask for his name and phone number. Explain this will allow someone to call to remind him to vote on election day. Ask questions directly from the canvass card (see Figure 12.1).
- If the canvass takes place before the deadline for voter registration, ask supporters if all eligible supporters in the household are registered to vote. If not, provide information on where and how to register and the deadline for registration.
- If the resident indicates he supports the bond but may have trouble getting to the polls, make a note on the canvass card that baby-sitting service or a ride to the polling place may be needed.
- Conclusion: "We hope you plan to vote on (date). Your vote is essential to the success of the school bond. Do you have any questions about the election or the bond issue? Thank you very much."
- Answer all questions that you can. *If you are stumped, don't make something up.* Make a note on the canvass card and place it in a separate pile with cards that need follow-up responses. Following through makes a strong positive impression on the voter.
- Do not leave campaign literature in mail boxes. This is against U.S. Postal Service rules. If no one is home, note this on your canvass sheet/card and return later for a follow-up visit.

Make sure every canvasser has an ample supply of canvass cards or sheets. Each entry should look like the sample in Figure 12.1.

Don't be discouraged by bad weather. The worse it is outside, the more likely people will be home when you call on them. Canvass when people are most likely to be home—evenings and weekends. Check the calendar of local happenings and, sad to say, blockbuster TV events, to avoid canvassing on the days or evenings when people won't want to be interrupted.

```
Name_____
Address_____
Phone_____Precinct/ward_____
Contact made _____Not home _____
Follow-up call _____
# Eligible voters_____Registered?_____
SUPPORTER:    YES___NO___UNSURE_____
Brochure delivered?_____
Need ride?_____Time: _____
Baby-sitter?_____Time:_____
Comments/questions: _____
_____
_____
```

Figure 12.1. Sample Canvass Card

THE TELEPHONE CANVASS

If there is a shortage of volunteers, or if the school district is very large or spread out, a phone canvass may be your best option.

There are two disadvantages of phone canvassing. First, the impact of face-to-face contact is lost. Second, the campaign literature will not be systematically delivered into the hands of each potential voter.

That being said, canvassing by phone is still an effective way to discover supporters. The names and needs of supporters will still be plotted on the master list for that reminder call, card, or letter just before or on election day. A sample phone canvass script is provided in Figure 12.2.

GENERAL ADVICE FOR CANVASSERS

Be brief. You are interrupting the respondent. Don't intrude longer than necessary. Think efficiency. You have much ground to cover.

Always be positive, upbeat, and courteous. If contacts become rude or abusive, do not respond in kind. Politely thank them for their time and leave or ring off.

Never argue with or try to convince non-supporters to vote "yes." By this stage, most voters have already made up their minds. Your time is best spent visiting or calling as many people as possible.

Do not discuss side issues not related directly to the election. It wastes time and does not help the cause. For example, if asked about teachers' salaries, respond, "That issue is outside the scope of the referendum, and I don't have information to offer about it."

Name _____

Address _____

Phone _____

"Hello, my name is_____. I have volunteered to call on behalf of (committee
    name).
    Is this the (name) residence?"
"May we count on your support for the new (improved) school?"
    YES___ NO___ UNDECIDED___
If the response is negative, thank the person and end the call.
If the person is unfamiliar with the issue, give a brief description of the proposal.
If the response is positive, continue . . .
"Are you registered to vote?" YES_____ NO_____
If not, and there is still time to register, "The deadline to register is (date). You can regis-
    ter at (time, location). We hope you will please take the time to register and to vote.
    Your support is very important."
If registered,
"Will you need a ride to the polls?" YES_____ Time:_____ NO_____
"Will you need child care while you vote?" YES_____ Time: _____NO____
"Do you have any questions or comments about the election or the bond issue?"
Answer questions briefly. If you are not sure of answer, note questions. Separate forms
    that need a follow-up response and forward to the canvass coordinator.

Comments:_____

_____

_____

"Thank you for your time. We'll look forward to your vote on (election date) very much."

Figure 12.2.   Sample Phone Canvass Script

If you are asked a question you can't answer, don't make something up!
Make note of it on your canvass card/sheet. Tell the inquirer you're not sure, but
you'll get back to him with the answer. Then *follow through*. Contact the canvass coordinator for an accurate response. Quick personal attention makes a
very good impression. Forgetting to respond will have the opposite effect.

On your sheet/card, briefly record your impression of each contact's position. The results will be used to compile lists of supporters. These potential
"yes" voters will be contacted again on or before election day.

Finish your canvass promptly. This will allow the committee enough time
to compile lists for effective follow-up.

Divide "yes" and "no" and "follow-up questions" cards into separate piles
and turn them in to the canvass coordinator. Turn in your lists by the specified date.

If the task is too much for you, or if you have extra time, or if you find supporters who would like to help out, let the canvass coordinator know promptly.

WHAT TO DO WITH THE RESULTS

When the canvass results are in, the survey-canvass coordinator will turn over the names of all supporters and undecided respondents to the secretary-treasurer. These names will be added to or checked against the master list of supporters. All unanswered questions will be forwarded to the publicity manager for prompt response.

While you've got them, don't let those splendid volunteers off the hook. If they are willing to do more, tap them for duties during final campaign days and on election day. Ask them if they would be willing to hand deliver a final campaign letter to their canvass area residents on election eve, if necessary.

Sign up volunteers to make follow-up calls, hang posters, distribute campaign tokens and literature, display yard signs, write letters to the editor, drive voters to the polls, baby-sit while supporters vote, and act as poll watchers and couriers. There will be plenty of work to share among willing hands.

All potential "yes" voters will receive reminder letters, postcards, and/or calls shortly before or on election day (see chapter 11, The Campaign, and chapter 13, Election Day).

THE LAST WORD ON CANVASSING

Enlist as many volunteers as you can for this project to spread the effort. Look particularly for supporters who have a direct stake in the outcome of the election—parents of kids affected by the election outcome, teachers, and school administrators.

Keep the canvass period short so it doesn't drag out. Time it well so you'll have enough time before election day to compile a complete list of "yes" voters.

The canvass is not the time to educate voters. It's too late for that. It is the means by which you locate "yes" votes so they can be reminded and encouraged to go to the polls.

The committee has been working for months on this school bond project. Then along comes this huge job with a tight schedule. It's likely many committee members are thoroughly sick of the whole thing. You'll be sorely tempted to forego a canvass and hope the voters will do the right thing on election day.

Don't give in to this temptation. The canvass, and what you do with the information gleaned from it, can mean the difference between success and failure in close elections. *Remember, success comes in not how many supporters you have but in how many actually vote.*

A thorough canvass can yield very detailed information on voter support. This information allows you to focus on those supporters and convert that support into "yes" votes on election day.

It's said, "The devil is in the details." So is success.

13

Election Day

I know what you're thinking. You never thought you'd survive to see election day, but it's finally arrived. You're tired. You've talked yourselves blue for nearly a year. Everyone has heard your pitch. You've done your best. It's up to the voters now. They'll do what's right.

No way!

You can't rest now. Election day is the most important part. It's great to get citizens to support school improvement, but the job is not done until those supporters have placed their "yes" votes in the ballot box. In close contests, referendums can fly or fail as a result of the committee's effort on election day.

Today the committee will be busier than ever.

RADIO TALK SHOWS

Begin the day by monitoring local radio call-in talk shows. Last-minute arguments, rumors, and misinformation brought up by the opposition can be damaging if not quickly refuted (with tact and facts, of course!). Don't give up on a single wavering vote. This is also an opportunity to remind supporters to go to the polls.

Assign a knowledgeable, articulate committee member or volunteer to monitor each program. Set the phone speed-dial to that station. Have your short sound-bite sales pitch ready.

THE PHONE BANK

Fire up the campaign hot line. Volunteers will be on hand to answer last-minute questions or arrange rides to the polls or child care for voters. Later in the day, these phones will be used to call the identified supporters who have not yet voted.

CAMPAIGN ETIQUETTE

It may seem like an opportunity too sweet to pass up, but refrain from placing any campaign literature or people near polling places. It is illegal to campaign within 100 feet of a polling place. This means no signs, posters, campaign tokens, hats, balloons, or people handing out literature. This goes for the county clerk's office during absentee or early voting.

POLL WATCHING

When the polls open, poll watchers are in place. The poll watcher does more than just stand around and watch. He notes on his copy of the master list each identified supporter as he casts his ballot. The watcher then periodically contacts the phone bank to report the no-show supporters. Poll watchers must not make any show of support for the bond, either by word, dress, or deed.

Each polling place should have at least one watcher. Schedule the poll watchers to work in shifts. The polls will be open a long time.

If no public phone is available at a given polling place, arrange for runners to collect the names of those who haven't voted yet and relay the information to the phone bank.

REMINDER CALLS

Phone volunteers will call all identified supporters who have not yet voted to remind them to do so. Spread these lists of tardy voters among as many phone volunteers as you can. This is a last-minute pitch, and time is running out. Have all callers use a short prepared script so there will be no fumbling. Make these calls upbeat and courteous, but get the point across to each supporter that his vote is crucial to success.

Every vote counts, so make it as easy as possible for supporters to cast them. Callers should offer last-minute rides and/or baby-sitting to supporters who otherwise would not be able to make it to the polls.

Keep at it. Call identified supporters until the last possible moment they can reach the polls before closing time. Don't give up on a single supporter while there is still time to get to the polls. That one missed vote could be the one that puts the referendum over the top.

TIMING THE ELECTION

What is the best time for a school bond election? The consensus is there is no best time. Much research has been done on the timing of elections, but bonds have passed and failed year-round.

The school board sets the date for the election. If the committee has a say in timing the election, be sensitive to your community's particular situation and use common sense:

- Don't hold the election close to a major holiday. People are too busy and distracted, and many travel away from home. A few weeks before Christmas might be a good time. The spirit of giving might grip otherwise Scrooge-like voters. Right after the Christmas holidays is *not* a good time. That's when the reality of the holiday bills sets in.
- Avoid summer vacation time for the election. The strongest group of school supporters are parents with school-age children. Make sure they are around to cast their votes.
- Around April 15 is a bad time. People are cranky and in no mood to increase their taxes.
- Allow some time for the dust to settle after a major school district reorganization or shake-up. Voters sometimes resist making too many changes in too short a time.
- The referendum *will* have a better chance of success if you go with a single-issue special election. If the referendum is not competing for attention with other issues, you will be able to focus voter attention exclusively on this one important matter.

There are several good reasons to avoid including the school referendum with local, state, and national elections. Many political campaigns today are conducted in a negative and mean-spirited way. By the end of a long, nasty campaign, many voters are angry and disappointed. Mud-slinging candidates can create a sour feeling among voters that can spill over and foul the school bond effort. If the school bond initiative runs alongside candidates who extol lower taxes, inadvertently they are campaigning against the bond.

Having read all that, don't worry too much about timing the election. What will carry the day in a school bond effort is research, planning, organization, and hard work.

14

After the Election

Intelligence is proved not by ease of learning, but by understanding what we learn.

Joseph Whitley

Between the time when the polls close and when the results become clear is the most anxious, suspenseful time for all committee members, volunteers, and supporters. This is not the evening for any committee member to stay home alone biting his nails.

THROW A PARTY—WIN, LOSE, OR DRAW

All committee members should plan on getting together on election night. Win, lose, or draw, throw a party for yourselves. If you've won, you should celebrate together. If you've lost, you can support one another in a big group cry.

Invite all volunteers and major supporters. Don't neglect to include veterans of previous successful or failed bond attempts. You learned from their successful techniques and painful mistakes. You began your effort by standing on their shoulders.

Throw a potluck dinner or bring party snacks. Bring cards and board games and music to help pass the time until the election results are known.

As the results start rolling in from the various precincts, post them on a chalk or bulletin board.

Assign one cool, articulate committee member to talk to the media. This will prevent crossed signals and confusion.

149

If election results show you have won, please leave your host's house or the meeting hall intact. Don't drive around noisily blowing your car horns. Flaunting victory is for high school football games. If you've lost, don't rend your clothes or burn down an "ugly's" house. Passing around sour grapes is poor manners.

Either way, make preparations for the morning after.

THE MORNING AFTER

Promptly remove all signs of the campaign. Pull down posters, pull up yard signs, take down ribbon, and so on. Campaign literature quickly turns into litter, which reflects badly on the committee.

In victory or defeat, show your appreciation for everyone's hard work and dedication. Everyone appreciates recognition, which may make them more willing to come back for more if necessary.

Think of ways to warmly and promptly thank everyone who had even the slightest hand in supporting the project. If your town is small, take the time to sit down and write a thank-you letter to each volunteer. If thanking each person individually is too big a task, thank everyone in a letter to the editor or take out a paid ad in the next newspaper after the election.

Remember, after election day there is still a community out there. There will be pockets of hard feelings on the losing side. Be gracious in victory or graceful in defeat. No bragging! No sour grapes! Being a poor winner or loser is unseemly and will stiffen opposition to the next attempt.

Win or lose, sooner or later there *will* be another school bond proposal. If the campaign was waged as war, it was a civil war. Take great pains not to create lifelong opponents. Remember, someone, maybe even you, will have to travel down this same road again someday.

WRAPPING THINGS UP

The committee's job is not complete until the paperwork is done. Before the committee disbands, you must prepare the groundwork for the next school bond campaign.

Hold one last committee meeting to analyze the bond effort from beginning to end. What would you have done differently? What activities would you emphasize more? Which were a waste of time? Which were your brilliant moments? What were your biggest blunders?

Ask the volunteers and canvassers for comments and suggestions. Where did they run into difficulties? Who provided unforeseen help? How might they have been more effective?

Collect copies of all materials: research of previous campaigns, the action plan in its many renditions, the audiovisual presentation, brochures, posters, and campaign tokens. Include photos of yard signs and billboards.

Gather copies of all news releases, articles, columns, flyers, brochures, newsletters, advertisements, scripts, and survey and canvass forms. Include all ambassador club briefing book materials and handouts.

Carefully store your master list of volunteers and supporters. List all those groups and individuals who donated cash, goods, or services and how much was contributed. Compile a comprehensive list of all endorsements and testimonials. Chances are many of these patrons will support the next school bond attempt.

Write up a narrative about the opposition. Be specific. What were the major arguments against the bond? Who were the main opponents? What did they do to try to defeat the bond measure?

Examine voter turnout. In which precincts/neighborhoods/areas was support weak and where was it strong? On a map of the district, plot voting margins by precinct.

If you have an ounce of energy left, and/or two dimes to rub together, conduct a post-election voter survey. This can be very useful, especially if the bond measure was defeated. Ask voters why they believe the school bond failed to pass. What would it take to convince them to support the next one?

Put all this information in a scrapbook. This material will prove priceless in the next campaign. Regardless of the outcome of this one, one thing is certain. Sooner or later all this information will come in very handy.

Compiling a scrapbook might seem rather obvious. But after the election the committee will be so sick and tired of the whole thing, your inclination will be to throw all that old junk out and get on with your lives. If you do, you condemn the next committee to wasting a lot of time and energy reinventing the wheel.

This is also the time for the committee to do some long-range planning and to make recommendations to the school board. Has the campaign revealed that the school district needs a public relations facelift? Do the schools need to develop a more prominent, positive image in the community?

Recommendations might include ways to showcase the schools:

- Take the schools to the community in positive ways, such as student community service projects and volunteer work.

- Invite the public into the schools with band concerts, science and cultural fairs, bazaars, and festivals.
- If senior citizen support is weak, have students do something nice for seniors. Organize a grandparents' day at school. Have the schools take musical and drama performances to the senior center.
- Develop liaison with the local media. Never pass up an opportunity to show off the schools' accomplishments and awards to the community.

Do not delay in compiling this scrapbook and making these recommendations. If you wait too long to complete this final task, fresh ideas and painful mistakes will fade. Important lessons will be lost. Committee members will quickly want to return to their normal lives, so strike while the iron is hot.

WHAT TO DO IF YOU LOSE

It is heartbreaking to lose a school bond election. You would not have started this project if the need had not been great. Now all that work was for nothing . . .

To maintain the enthusiasm and confidence necessary to run an effective campaign, committees members must assume the school bond will pass. Having given little thought to losing, the reality of defeat at the polls can catch you unprepared.

It is not uncommon for people to take rejection of a bond as a personal rejection, much as an artist can be hurt by criticism of his sculpture or painting. Try not to despair. As hard as it is to lose, it is not a personal repudiation. Whatever their reasons, the voters rejected the bond issue, not you as a person.

Nor is losing the end of the world. Never feel all that work was for nothing. Many bond issues must be placed before the voters several times before they finally pass. Try to think of the loss as a setback along the road to success. The need for school improvement has not gone away. Your effort has helped pave the way for a successful bond election next time.

Take a break, take a deep breath, dust yourselves off, and get ready to try again.

15

Conclusion

Studies have shown that a citizens' action committee strongly boosts school bond success. If the committee forms early, is highly organized, and stays focused and committed for the long haul, the chance of success is better yet. The most successful campaigns concentrate on educational needs of students. Thorough research into past attempts, long-range planning, tight organization, and spirited public relations are crucial.

Here are a few last bits of advice.

ALL IS PERCEPTION

Most people make decisions based on emotion rather than logic. The facts will always take a back seat to people's feelings. To ignore the opinions and wishes of the people is to beg for defeat. First appeal to their emotions, then press your case with facts.

Don't try to push through or go around strongly held beliefs, no matter how dumb or invalid they are. Voters may not admit to a bias, but that bias will show up in the ballot box.

For example, say the school administrators believe their greatest need is a 15,000-square-foot warehouse. Reams of paper are stacked in the halls at the district office, and there is nowhere to stash supplies. A new warehouse would streamline distribution and minimize loss, damage, and theft.

But how do the voters feel about building a new warehouse? Chances are they neither know nor care about the district's storage problems. Most people will be concerned only with the condition of the school as it relates to the students. Are there enough teachers, books, and classroom space? Does the roof leak on the children's heads in class? Therefore, your pitch to the public will concentrate on the shortcomings of classroom facilities and minimize the need for more storage.

Another example: two months before the school bond election, the school board approves the installation of an underground sprinkler system in the high school football field. It will cost $30,000. The public is furious about this "frivolous" waste of tax dollars.

The superintendent explains that it is actually a long-term savings in time, effort, and money. The money comes out of the grounds and maintenance fund, not general operating funds. But all the public sees, right before a major bond asking, is the equivalent of one teacher's yearly salary buried in the ground. Technically the superintendent is right—dead right.

Another example: many people believe major power lines are hazardous to health. Scientific research has failed to prove any link, but nothing will sway this popular belief. If you choose a site for the new elementary school that is too close to a major power line, even if it is the best all-around site, you may be taking on a grave handicap. People will declare their support for a new school, but their feelings about electromagnetic radiation will be reflected in the final vote tally.

FINAL WORDS

A school bond effort is long, hard, and grueling work. If it is to succeed, committee members must dream, live, and breathe school improvement for many months. Pace yourself. A school bond effort is a marathon, not a sprint.

You must bring passion to the project, not ego. You must have strong feelings but not show them. You must possess patience, a ready smile, and a thick skin. Once the committee takes on an official presence, the face you show the community must be optimistic and open—a solid image of trust and truth.

Conduct the campaign as though you expect to win. You can only succeed if the public assumes you will. You are on the high road. You are the good guys. You are working for the children to improve the schools and thereby your community.

No insult or argument can defeat a good idea whose time has come.

Keep your eye on the prize. Don't allow distractions, side issues, or personal problems to divert you from the issue—school improvement.

Never complain or whine in public.

Learn to trust and rely on your committee members. Early on you will learn which members are rock-solid reliable and which are less so, who are the doers and who are the talkers. Go easy on the latter. Remember, you are all volunteers. Some will promise more of themselves than they are able to give. Some well-meaning people can't say "no" when they really should. Be content with what help you get, and cheerfully work around the empty promises.

Trust your community. Listen carefully to what people say. How far are they willing to go to improve the school? How much are they willing to spend? Precious few cities or towns are rolling in dough. Keep that firmly in mind as you help design and plan the project. You can only ride the bus in the direction it's going. To request too much or ask for things the voters find unacceptable is to invite failure.

Work smart. Trying to do too much yields about the same results as doing too little, but it costs more. Choose activities that will give you the most "bang for your buck," the widest exposure.

Don't be too hard on yourselves when you make those inevitable mistakes or miss a prime opportunity. There will be more mistakes where those came from. Learn from them to avoid repeating them.

Don't be shy about reaching out for help or advice. Gather as many volunteers as you can. Make each one feel like a valued team member, and keep them actively engaged. Give them meaningful work to do. Remember, each volunteer is a "yes" vote.

Be ever alert for helping hands from unexpected places, not just the usual ones. Always be prepared to take advantage of happy turns of events.

Many school bond elections do not pass on the first try. If you lose, don't despair. You have laid a healthy foundation for the next time around. If the need for school improvement is great, if you work hard, and if you are true to your cause and truthful with your community, then you will prevail—if not the first time, then the next or the next.

It is human nature to hold permanent grudges over the tiniest slights and insults. Go to great lengths to avoid creating them. Make every effort to leave the community in at least as healthy an emotional condition as you found it when you started. That way, win, lose, or draw, you all win.

Keep your chin up. Hang on to your sense of humor. You won't make it without it.

In Lewis Carroll's *Alice in Wonderland*, the Red Queen advised Alice, "Start at the beginning, go through to the end and then stop." After the election is over, after you've compiled your scrapbook and thanked the community for its support, *stop*. Pull out those barbs and drop them. Rub out those bruises and let them fade away. Take off your school improvement committee hat and rejoin the real world.

Your quest will lead you to a thorough understanding of human nature—sweet and mean. You will learn the true meaning of apathy, willful ignorance, generosity, and kindness. You will discover that most people are optimistic and reasonable.

Your reward may be a new or improved school, but that's not all. You will find talents and confidence in yourself you may not know you have. Success builds community pride, which leads to other successes. It shows the community that working together can produce mutual benefits. That can become habit-forming.

Is it time? If you're sure it's past time to improve that old school or build a new one, go for it.

Are you ready? Of course not!

But as Cardinal Richard Cushing said, "The fact is, that to do anything in the world worth doing, we must not stand back shivering and thinking of the cold and danger, but jump in and scramble through as well as we can."

Good luck!

Appendix A

Countdown to Election Day

12 MONTHS BEFORE ELECTION DAY:
- ❏ Call public meeting and collect the names of supporters who attend.
- ❏ Organize citizens' committee.

11 MONTHS BEFORE ELECTION DAY: INFORMATION PHASE
- ❏ Develop questionnaire and survey community.
- ❏ Report the results to the community and the school board.
- ❏ Begin research of previous school bond attempts.
- ❏ Begin focus group meetings (ambassadors club).
- ❏ Begin collecting names of supporters.

8 MONTHS BEFORE ELECTION DAY: EDUCATION PHASE
- ❏ Produce video or other audiovisual presentation.
- ❏ Continue ambassadors club focus group meetings.
- ❏ Have publicity subcommittee members produce newsletters, newspaper columns, news releases, and public service announcements.
- ❏ Sponsor community events and fund raising activities.
- ❏ Work with the school board (architect) on needs and design of school improvement.
- ❏ Collect names and pledges of support from registered voters and business, civic, and political leaders.
- ❏ Design and produce or order campaign tokens, signs, and so on.

1 MONTH BEFORE ELECTION DAY: CAMPAIGN PHASE
- ❏ Continue ambassadors club activities.
- ❏ Have publicity subcommittee members organize paid ads, letters to the editor, photo opportunities with community leaders, and committee-sponsored events.

❑ Have publicity manager buy newspaper space and schedule endorsements and ads.

❑ Distribute and display campaign brochure, tokens, posters, yard signs, and so on.

❑ Make reminder calls and/or send letters to supporters to "get out and vote."

❑ Canvass voters and tabulate supporters.

❑ Hold a special voter registration day.

ELECTION DAY
❑ Begin poll watching.

❑ Monitor and respond to local radio talk shows.

❑ Activate phone bank to remind supporters to vote.

❑ Provide rides for supporters to the polls.

❑ Throw a win, lose, or draw party.

POST-ELECTION CHORES
❑ Remove all campaign literature—posters, yard signs, ribbon, placards, and so on.

❑ Publicly thank all volunteers and supporters.

❑ Pay all debts and file campaign finance forms with appropriate government agencies.

❑ Take post-election survey.

❑ Analyze election results by precinct and neighborhood.

❑ Compile scrapbook.

❑ Join your real life in progress.

Appendix B

Sample Formats, Letters, and Poems

Here is a collection of standard formats, sample forms, questionnaires, etc. Modify them to suit your needs.

SAMPLE INTRODUCTORY LETTER TO SIGNATURE POSTER

This letter can be used in conjunction with the signature poster. It would appear in the daily newspaper on the final day before the election or the final weekly edition.

Open Letter from Citizens:

We believe this bond issue is a necessary project now. Our school system genuinely needs additional space to continue to provide the highest-quality education for our young citizens.

This progressive step will (give a brief description of the project). This project shows a strong commitment to the future of our children and our community.

As supporters of the bond issue, we want to thank each of you for your interest in this important decision. We hope you will arrive at the same decision we have and vote "yes" on Tuesday.

(List of names of supporters follows.)

SAMPLE NEWS RELEASE

FROM:	K.I.D.S. Committee	For Immediate Release
CONTACT:	Ms. Story Teller,	(or) For Release on (date)
	Publicity Manager	
	(999) 123-4567	
DATE:	July 23, 20XX	

SCHOOL BOARD MEMBERS
VOLUNTEER FOR DUNKING BOOTH

Yourtown, State—Four members of the Yourtown School Board plan to show their support for the proposed school bond by volunteering to be dunked during the 25th Annual Summerfest, July 8, 9, and 10.

John Green, Joe Blue, Tom Red, and Paul Revere have signed on for one hour each at the dunking booth, beginning Friday at 1 PM. The booth is located in the community pavilion.

The dunking booth is sponsored by the K.I.D.S. Committee, a citizens' group promoting the proposed $12 million school bond. Funds raised at the booth will help the committee's efforts.

If successful, the bond will fund a new elementary school on the north side of town and a new science wing of three new classrooms at the middle school.

"We don't mind making fools of ourselves if it will help our schools," Revere said. "I just hope the weather is warm."

"I know there are plenty of people who would like to dunk us," Green said. "This is their big chance, and it's for a good cause."

About the K.I.D.S. Committee: The Keep Improving District Schools (K.I.D.S.) Committee formed last November to seek community consensus on ways to improve school facilities in Yourtown public schools. The committee members have surveyed district voters and worked with the school board to prepare the proposed school referendum.

The school bond vote will be held Tuesday, September 12.

For more information about the committee or the school bond, call K.I.D.S. Committee co-chairs Ms. Story Teller at 123-4567 or Jack No Itall at 345-6789.

SAMPLE NEWSPAPER COLUMN AND/OR NEWSLETTER TOPICS

Information Phase:

- Introduction of the committee: Who we are and what we hope to accomplish
- Survey: What it is, why we are doing it, and when to expect it
- Results of the survey

Education Phase:

- Focus groups: We're coming around to see you. What we hope to accomplish
- Video: Describe production and how you plan to use it
- Current school situation: Buildings, maintenance, costs
- Health, safety, access
- Life in the portable classrooms
- History: History of the school(s) and the results of past school bond referendums
- Teachers: How they are doing a fine job in less than ideal conditions
- Seniors and non-parents: Why we must all support children's education today
- Just folks: Importance of education in a democratic society
- Schools are the heart and soul of the community
- Essential that our children have modern education to do well in the 21st century
- Possible new school sites: Distance to school, busing
- Private school and public schools working together
- The spirit of compromise

Campaign Phase:

- The school: Describe the planned improvements
- Pros and cons of selected site—why it was chosen
- The bond: Cost, valuation, length
- Children's essay contest
- The community: How new school will benefit families, business, community pride
- The elderly: It is your duty and responsibility to help provide for the next generation . . .
  - Someone provided you with a good school . . .
  - Services and facilities for the elderly provided by the community
- Poetry

All Phases:

Conclude each article by inviting everyone to attend all activities, meetings, and events.

SAMPLE PUBLIC SERVICE ANNOUNCEMENT

Double-space the text and type in all capital letters. Spell everything out to avoid confusion. Keep it short, but try to mention essential information at least twice.

FROM: K.I.D.S. Committee   For Immediate Release
CONTACT: Story Teller,   (or) For Release on (date)
                Publicity Manager
                (999) 123-4567
DATE: June 23, 20XX

COME DUNK THE SCHOOL BOARD!

COME DUNK YOUR FAVORITE SCHOOL BOARD MEMBER AT THE SUMMERFEST CARNIVAL THIS SATURDAY AND SUNDAY AFTERNOON.

FOUR MEMBERS OF THE YOURTOWN PUBLIC SCHOOL DISTRICT BOARD OF EDUCATION HAVE VOLUNTEERED TO GET SOAKED IN THE DUNKING BOOTH. PROCEEDS WILL SUPPORT THE K.I.D.S. COMMITTEE'S EFFORTS TO IMPROVE OUR SCHOOL.

DON'T MISS THE FUN AT THE CITY PAVILION THIS SATURDAY AND SUNDAY FROM 1 TO 5 PM.

SAMPLE FLYER

This half-page flyer can be dropped into grocery bags at the local store, slipped into monthly utility bills mailed to customers, or left as handouts on the sales counters of supporting businesses.

TOP TEN REASONS TO SUPPORT THE BOND ISSUE

10. The alternative school has a waiting list of over 300 applicants but has space for only 70.
9. We need to improve our educational facilities to provide modern opportunities for every student.
8. The proposed location for the new school lies in the path of future residential growth.
7. The current school holds 700 students in a school designed for 550 students.
6. According to a recent survey, 74 percent of the citizens polled believe improvement in the school system is needed.
5. Since 1995, school enrollment in District 7 has increased by 750 students—which is approximately the size of the proposed middle school.
4. The old school does not meet federally mandated handicapped access requirements.
3. The old school does not meet current fire- and life-safety regulations.
2. The new school will cost the average homeowner the daily cost of a cup of coffee.
1. The new school will attract business and prospective employees. It will be a facility in which the community can be proud.

For the sake of our children and our community, please support the school bond on Tuesday, March 1, 20XX.

SAMPLE FOCUS GROUP MEETING HANDOUT

POSITIVE AND NEGATIVE ASPECTS
OF THE THREE MOST POPULAR PROPOSED SCHOOL SITES
Based on phone survey, conducted April 20XX

Positive	Negative
Present Location	
• Central location	• Limited room for expansion
• Shared lunch program convenient to parochial school	• Lunch program disrupted for estimated 18 months during construction
• No contact with high school students	• Two-story building must meet Disabilities Act requirements (elevator)
• District owns land	• Reduced playground space
	• Displacement of children for estimated 18 months
	• Hazard—drop off areas
Next to High School	
• Central location in town	• Limited site expansion
• Adequate play area	• Contact of high school and grade school students (could be reduced by scheduling changes)
• Elementary gym closer to high school	• Heavier traffic, narrow streets
• One-story school	• Major power lines near school (Hazard? Added expense to move them?)
• Elementary parking shared with high school	• Shared cafeteria high school/elementary
• Good walking/bicycle access	• Disruption/safety of high school students during construction
• Shared athletic fields	
• District owns land	
New Site North of Town	
• Adequate space available	• Only light duty streets for auto access
• Residential/light traffic	• Disruption of residential neighborhood
• Good access for walking and bicycling	• Not very central location
• Future residential development around school	• Street, utility extensions
• Room for expansion	• District must purchase land
• Good access to city ball fields	
• One-story school	

SAMPLE AUDIOVISUAL PRODUCTION

Here is a sample format of two pages of audiovisual script. On the left are the video shots you want, and on the right is the narrative.
Estimated Time: 13 Minutes; Should Not Exceed 15 Minutes

VIDEO	AUDIO
Business District Hospital City Park	Yourtown is a wonderful place to live. We have a lively business community and excellent health care facilities. It is a pleasant, safe place to raise our children. But the community has one profound weakness . . .
Crowded playground with 1913 building in background Adult entering school	Our elementary school. It is neither safe nor pleasant. We'd like to take you on a tour of the school.
1913 Building 1938 Addition 1955 Addition Portable buildings on 4th Street Portable buildings at high school	Yourtown Elementary School includes 11 separate buildings at 2 locations. The three main buildings were built in 1913, 1938, and 1955. Eight portable buildings were added in 1989. Kindergarten through fourth graders attend school in seven buildings on 4th Street. Fifth and sixth graders attend class next to the high school in four portable units. Minutes:seconds elapsed time this page > <u>00:58</u> Minutes:seconds total so far > 00:58

continued

PRODUCTION: SCHOOL TOUR   Page 2 of 15

VIDEO	AUDIO
Children entering class Children hanging coats Children taking seats	Children were moved into the portables after the 1913 building was condemned by the fire marshal. Each portable unit is 28 feet by 54 feet. There are two classrooms per portable. The average classroom size is 540 square feet. The state recommends a classroom size of at least 700 square feet.
Curtain dividing classroom	The fire code requires two exits, so each class exits into the other. There is no soundproofing between the two classrooms. Each class is noisy and confusing because sight and sound carries easily between them. [Voice over classroom sounds]
Bathroom facilities	An average of 45 children share two small bathrooms. The bathrooms double as storage rooms.
Kids putting on coats, lining up, walking, and entering music portable	The children travel outside many times each day to go to the library, physical education, music, lunch, and special classes. An estimated five to six days of learning time each year is wasted dressing, lining up, and going to and from activities in other rooms.

<u>00:86</u>
01:44

. . . and so on. Make sure the title and page number is printed on the top of every page.

SAMPLE LETTER TO COLLEGE STUDENTS

Dear (personalize this if possible),

The students of (your town) need your help. On (election date if it has been set), the citizens of (your town) will vote on a ($$) school bond. If approved, the bond funds will be used (briefly describe the project).

As recent graduates, no one knows better than you how badly our community needs this school improvement. Now you have the opportunity to make a difference. Your vote of support will help the students of (your town) to have the kind of school you wish you'd had.

If you are not registered to vote, you can do so by filling out and returning the enclosed form in the enclosed envelope before (deadline).

If you will be away from home on election day, you can use the enclosed form to request an absentee ballot.

Please take the time to register—and to vote "yes"—for school improvement in the upcoming school bond election.

Sincerely,

/s/

Inky Penn, Secretary

(Your name) Committee

Address

Contact phone number

Check with your local registrar to ensure you offer students the correct forms and procedure. Give students plenty of time to respond before the deadline for registration/absentee ballot application.

SAMPLE OPEN LETTER FROM THE
COMMITTEE TO THE COMMUNITY
(Printed in the Final Newspaper before Election Day)

Patrons of School District X:

The (your name) Committee wishes to thank everyone for the warm and enthusiastic support we have received during our quest for a new (improved) school.

We are a volunteer group consisting of your neighbors, friends, and associates. Our goal has been to find out what the community needs and wants in (your project) and then work toward that end. You have generously responded with encouragement, suggestions, and constructive criticism.

Our initial survey showed that the large majority of citizens (X percent) believe something must be done to improve our school(s). The committee worked long and hard to find out what that "something" should be and to submit a proposal that will fit (your town's) long-term needs.

We have tried to be as open, honest, and forthright as possible in every aspect of this campaign. Happily, the community has responded in kind.

We realize that what we are working toward will involve higher taxes, but we believe this is an excellent investment for our town to make. Just as forward-thinking citizens long ago paid for our current school facilities, so, too, must we invest in the generations to come.

If the design and the site are not exactly what each individual has in mind, we ask only that you consider compromise. In any group of any size, if we insist on getting only our own way, we may end up with nothing at all.

By approving this bond issue, we will improve our schools for the benefit of the children of District X and for the progress of our community.

We Urge You to Lend Your Support by Voting "Yes" on (date).

Paid for by (Your committee name), Money Baggs, Treasurer

- If you would plan for a year, plant a crop.
- If you would plan for 10 years, plant a tree.
- If you would plan for 100 years, build a school.

SAMPLE SCHOOL BOARD LETTER

This letter should be printed as a newspaper ad. It must be paid for personally by the school board members, not with public/school funds. Be sure this is noted at the bottom of the ad.

A STATEMENT FROM THE DISTRICT X BOARD OF EDUCATION

(Date) is a very important day for our community. A special school bond proposal will be presented to you, the voters. Approval of the bond will allow us to build (briefly describe project) for the children of (your town).

Your board has studied the problem of our aging (crowded, etc.) facilities for several years. We believe the current proposal is a very good long-term solution to our facility problems.

As taxpayers of District X, we, too, are concerned about costs. We believe our children are receiving very high-quality education. We also believe that they deserve modern facilities, which will allow them suitable training for life and work in the 21st century.

Help us to maintain the quality of education that prevails in our schools. Please vote YES in the upcoming bond issue election on (date).

Sincerely,
/s/
All school board members

HOW MUCH IS ONE VOTE WORTH?

In 1645, one vote gave Oliver Cromwell control of England.

In 1649, one vote caused Charles I of England to be executed.

In 1776, one vote gave America the English language instead of German.

In 1845, one vote brought Texas into the Union.

In 1846, one vote brought Oregon Territory under American control.

In 1868, one vote saved President Andrew Johnson from removal from office.

In 1876, one vote changed France from a monarchy to a republic.

In 1876, one vote gave Rutherford B. Hayes the presidency of the United States.

In 1933, one vote gave Adolph Hitler leadership of the Nazi Party.

In 1960, one vote change in each precinct in Illinois would have denied John F. Kennedy the presidency.

March Fong Eu
California Secretary of State, 1984

UNDER ONE ROOF

A house divided cannot stand
Of this history gives us ample proof.
Broken nations, however grand
Scattered; fall like castles made of sand.
Our school belongs under one roof.
Adults make mistakes from day to day
Of this history gives us ample proof.
If mistakes are made, I can only say
Children should not be the ones who pay.
Our school belongs under one roof.
What we do today, the future touches.
Of past investment we are the proof.
To paint the future as at us it rushes
Our children must serve as brushes.
Our school belongs under one roof.

Denis Kaeding, principal
O'Neill (Nebraska) Elementary School

Appendix C

Sample Letters to the Editor

Letters to the editor can have a large impact on the electorate. They are the ultimate grassroots activity—citizens speaking directly to citizens.

A short, concise letter has more impact than a long, wordy one. Try to address one topic only in each letter.

To get the creative juices flowing and to be sure to cover several topics without overlap, host a "Letter to the Editor" writing party. Or find someone with a way with words to ghostwrite letters to be signed and submitted by various supporters.

Ask your local newspaper for its requirements for submitting letters to the opinion/editorial page. Stay within the paper's guidelines of length and format. On each letter, be sure to include the name, address, and telephone number of the "writer." The paper will not publish letters without this information.

Here are some sample letters covering different aspects of a typical bond issue.

Dear Editor:

Are we willing to follow in the footsteps of our ancestors? They made large sacrifices to ensure a quality education for their children. They built the schools we now use. Where would we be without them?

But our schools are showing their age. They are overcrowded, outdated, dangerous, and unpleasant.

In this electronic age, with all its complexities and challenges, we cannot properly prepare our children for tomorrow in the schools they are using today.

continued

---

continued

Let's make a few sacrifices today to guarantee a better future for our young people. Let's discard shortsightedness and selfishness and choose community service. Make a difference and vote "yes" on the school bond.

The following letter can be circulated among the religious community for signatures.

Dear Editor:

The following members of the Yourtown Ministerial Association voice their support for the upcoming school bond measure. We ask the voters to join us in making certain our children have safe and modern facilities in which to learn.

Let us love our children by helping them to develop all of the gifts that God has given them.

/s/   Rev. John Smith
         Rev. James Jones
         Pastor John Doe

This letter can have an impact on the business community.

Dear Editor:

The (Ourtown) Board of Economic Development (or Jaycees or Chamber of Commerce) endorses the upcoming school bond measure.

Surveys tell us that school quality is one of the top concerns of businesses that plan to relocate. Realtors tell us that the condition of the local schools is one of the first questions they are asked by prospective home buyers.

Overcrowded and outdated schools are seen as a real negative in the economic health of any community. They may cause some businesses and top-notch employees to pass (Ourtown) by. We can't afford to lose potential business and jobs in our community.

School improvement is badly needed. Having quality educational facilities here may be the single most important factor in the economic development of our county.

Providing (Ourtown's) children with a quality education is the best investment we can make in our own future. We must ensure they are well prepared for higher education and higher-paying jobs in the 21st century.

This letter expresses the views of current high school students.

Dear Editor:

"We raised our kids, you raise your kids. I'm not paying any more taxes for schools."

This shortsighted, narrow voice of self-interest fortunately did not prevail when my parents were children. My parents pay property taxes and so do my grandparents. Their schools had well-lighted classrooms, gymnasiums, a cafeteria, and playground equipment.

We know that our elders do not enjoy digging deeper for the money to improve our schools. But they must know that educating our town's children is a kind of social insurance. Our founding fathers knew that the best protection of democracy is a good education.

Times have changed. Unfortunately the facilities in our school have become run-down, outdated, overcrowded, unsafe, and unhealthy. Our parents' generation is the last one that will be employable without being computer-literate. There are so many more opportunities and pitfalls available for today's graduates.

Someday soon we will graduate, start jobs and families, and begin paying taxes ourselves. We will repay our debt by funding modern school facilities for future generations. The student of the past owes it to the student of the future. That's how it works.

Please vote "Yes" on Tuesday.

/s/ Student(s)

Dear Editor:

I remember my mom and dad discussing a bond issue during the Great Depression. "We'll manage somehow. We have to see the young people get a good education. They are the future of this country."

We citizens forget this attitude at our own peril. If this country is to compete with the rest of the world, we had better equip our young people with the wherewithal to do it.

Dear Editor:

For (X) years, my family and I have been pleased to call (Ourtown) our home. It's been a great place to live, work, and raise a family.

continued

continued

There's one need, however, that our community has failed to address for too long—the lack of a decent school facility for our young people.

I am convinced that for the future welfare of our community as a whole, including its businesses, churches, and other institutions, we must have a school system that will attract and retain the kind of families that will continue to make (Ourtown) a great place to live. If we want to continue to be the shopping, business, and medical center of our region—facilities that we ALL need—it's important that we offer educational opportunities that are second to none.

Will it be cheap? Of course not. Will it ever get cheaper? Not likely. Had we approved the first school bond proposal we'd already have a new school, and at much less than the cost of the present proposal.

Now is the time to act. As a homeowner and taxpayer, I urge all of you to ensure the future of (Ourtown) by voting "yes" for a new school on (date).

Let's do something positive for our community and for our children.

Dear Editor:

Why should the elderly who have retired here have to pay to support a school system they do not use? It is hard to understand the logic of such thinking.

First, all of us, young and old, are a part of this community. We enjoy the benefits of it, and we must all support it. How much of my tax money goes to support the Senior Center or Meals on Wheels?

Second, the children in our schools are the backbone and the future of this community. If youngsters do not receive a good education, there will be no future.

Don't care about the future? As long as you are alive and living in a community, you are a part of it and have a responsibility to it. If you are not generous in spirit, how can you expect others to be kind and generous in return?

Give the future a break. If one expects the younger generation to look up to, respect, and seek advice from its elders, then those elders must set a good example. Then maybe our future leaders will do the same when it's their turn.

This letter addresses the cost of a school bond . . .

Dear Editor:
    It has been suggested that governments, like individuals, should pay for large public works projects by saving up the money for them to avoid paying "unnecessary interest."
    It's good advice for citizens to pay as we go for most purchases, but how many citizens could ever save enough to buy big-ticket items such as homes or new cars or to start a new business without financing them through mortgages and loans?
    In addition, unlike private citizens, governments work within the constraint of annual budgets—funds that cannot be saved or carried over to the following year. How could a government gather enough money in a single year to pay cash for a new school, upgrade water and sewer systems, or build new roads?
    Asking the public through bond referenda to borrow the money to fund these vital facilities is the only way public projects can be built.
    This town has gone far too long without a decent school for our children. It's time we pulled together and signed on the dotted line for school improvement.
    Vote "Yes" this Tuesday for a new elementary school.

These two final letters are pretty bristly. Use with caution.

Dear Editor:
    If our schools were prisons, we would be under court order to release our students because of overcrowding.
    What kind of a message are we sending to our young people? Let's treat our future leaders better than we treat our convicts. Please vote "yes" for the school bond measure on election day.

Dear Editor:

"I don't have any kids in that school. I don't want my taxes to go to educating somebody else's kids." Well, until you learn how to drill and fill your own teeth, concoct your own medicine, or generate your own electricity, you must depend on others to maintain a civilized lifestyle.

This means making sure that dentist, pharmacist, or electrical engineer gets a good start in life with a good education. That means replacing that dilapidated old schoolhouse. You owe it to yourself and to your community.

Vote "Yes" in the school bond election on Tuesday.

Appendix D

Sample Forms

VOTER REMINDER POSTCARD

These postcards or short letters should be sent right before the election and only to known supporters. You don't want to remind or motivate the opposition to vote.

The "picture" side of the postcard should include the committee's name and logo. A picture or drawing of kids or the architect's drawing of the proposed school is effective. Whatever you use, make it instantly recognizable and related to the school bond measure.

How much you are able to personalize the reminder (name of supporter, location of voting precinct) depends on the number of volunteers you have available. Don't worry, though, if the reminder must be generic. People generally know where they are supposed to vote.

Hello, (*Personalize if possible*)   STAMP
This is a reminder to vote in the upcoming (*Check on rates for bulk mail*)
school bond election.
Election date: Time:
Precinct/Location:

Committee name, logo

(*Make a short upbeat pitch for the bond.
Focus on the kids. Make every word count.*)

Name _____
Address _____

_____

If you need a ride to the polls or a baby-sitter
while you vote or other assistance, call
(committee member name and phone number).
We'll be happy to help. Thank you for your support.

(*Hand-signed cards will have more impact.*)

REMINDER TO REMINDER TO VOTE TELEPHONE SCRIPT

Name of supporter (list only if ride, etc., is needed):
Hello, this is (your name). I'm calling on behalf of (committee name). This is just a reminder to vote in the upcoming school bond election on (date). The polls will be open from ___to ___. Your polling place is (location/address). If you need a ride to the polls, a baby-sitter, or other help, I'll be happy to arrange it for you.
Baby-sitting:_____ Ride to polls:_____
Thanks for your time. See you at the polls.

ACTION PLANNING WORKSHEET
Objective:_____

Activity #1 _____
   In Charge:_____
   When: _____
   Resources Needed: _____
   $ _____

Activity #2
   In Charge:_____
   When: _____
   Resources Needed: _____
   $ _____

Activity #3 _____
   In Charge:_____
   When: _____
   Resources Needed: _____
   $ _____

Activity #4 _____
   In Charge:_____
   When: _____
   Resources Needed: _____
   $ _____

Activity #5 _____
   In Charge:_____
   When: _____
   Resources Needed: _____
   $ _____

Activity #6 _____
   In Charge:_____
   When: _____
   Resources Needed: _____
   $ _____

FOCUS GROUP MEETING LOG

The chief ambassador keeps this record. Use as cover sheet for focus group surveys for each meeting.

Date _____ How Many Attended? _____
Name of Group or Organization _____
Ambassadors: Presenter _____ Notetaker _____
Comments: _____
_____
_____

****

Date _____ How Many Attended? _____
Name of Group or Organization _____
Ambassadors: Presenter _____ Notetaker _____
Comments: _____
_____
_____

****

Date _____ How Many Attended? _____
Name of Group or Organization _____
Ambassadors: Presenter _____ Notetaker _____
Comments: _____
_____
_____

****

Date _____ How Many Attended? _____
Name of Group or Organization _____
Ambassadors: Presenter _____ Notetaker _____
Comments: _____
_____
_____

****

Date _____ How Many Attended? _____
Name of Group or Organization _____
Ambassadors: Presenter _____ Notetaker _____
Comments: _____
_____
_____

****

CHILDREN'S ESSAY ENTRY FORM

(Your Name) Committee Children's Essay Contest

This essay contest is open to all elementary school-age children. The essay theme is "Why a New School Will Be Good for Our Community" (*or whatever suits your situation. Keep it positive and focused on the school and children*).

Length for the first and second graders' essays will be a maximum of 100 words. The third through sixth grade essays should be 200 words or less.

First and second prizes will be awarded in each of three categories: Grades 1–2, Grades 3–4, and Grades 5–6.

- **First prize is . . .** (*Hit up local business supporters for savings bonds and gift certificates.*)
- **Second prize is . . .** (*Be sure to prominently list all prize donors. Write each donor a thank-you letter and/or thank each publicly with a letter to the editor.*)

Entries must be submitted by (date). They may be dropped off or mailed (where) . . .

Name: _____ Phone: _____

Address: _____

Grade in (school year) (check one): 1–2,_____3–4_____ 5–6_____

- Please attach this form to the <u>back</u> of the essay. Do not sign or place your name on the front page.
- Essays will be judged by (*some reputable literate person—English teacher? Newspaper editor?—and not a member of the committee*).
- Essays submitted for this contest may be included in promotional material by the (your) Committee.

STUDENT TRANSPORTATION SURVEY

This questionnaire must receive the blessing of the principal of each school before distribution to the teachers. It would be a good idea to deliver it to the principal for distribution and collection.

Teacher _____ Class _____ Grade _____

Dear Teacher (personalize if possible),

The (Your name) Committee is gathering information about how students arrive and depart from school. Please note your students' responses to the following questions:
By a show of hands,

How many students are driven *to* school 1 day per week? _____
2 days _____ 3 days _____ 4 days _____ Every day _____

How many students walk *to* school 1 day per week? _____
2 days _____ 3 days _____ 4 days _____ Every day _____

How many students ride the bus *to* school 1 day per week? _____
2 days _____ 3 days _____ 4 days _____ Every day _____

How many students are driven home *from* school 1 day per week? _____
2 days _____ 3 days _____ 4 days _____ Every day _____

How many students walk home *from* school 1 day per week? _____
2 days _____ 3 days _____ 4 days _____ Every day _____

How many students ride the bus home *from* school 1 day per week? _____
2 days _____ 3 days _____ 4 days _____ Every day _____

Thank you!
Please forward this survey to _____ by _____ (date)

SAMPLE CANVASS FORM

Print on single sheets or 3 × 5-inch cards—whatever is most convenient.

Name _____   Name _____
Address _____   Address _____
Phone _____ At home _____   Phone _____ At home _____
voters ____ Registered? _____   # voters ____ Registered? _____
Supporter? _____   Supporter? _____
Brochure delivered _____   Brochure delivered _____
Follow-up visit _____   Follow-up visit _____
Ride to polls ___ Baby-sitting ___   Ride to polls ___ Baby-sitting ___
Comments _____   Comments _____

Name _____   Name _____
Address _____   Address _____
Phone _____ At home _____   Phone _____ At home _____
voters ____ Registered? _____   # voters ____ Registered? _____
Supporter? _____   Supporter? _____
Brochure delivered _____   Brochure delivered _____
Follow-up visit _____   Follow-up visit _____
Ride to polls ___ Baby-sitting ___   Ride to polls ___ Baby-sitting ___
Comments _____   Comments _____

Name _____   Name _____
Address _____   Address _____
Phone _____ At home _____   Phone _____ At home _____
voters ____ Registered? _____   # voters ____ Registered? _____
Supporter? _____   Supporter? _____
Brochure delivered _____   Brochure delivered _____
Follow-up visit _____   Follow-up visit _____
Ride to polls ___ Baby-sitting ___   Ride to polls ___ Baby-sitting ___
Comments _____   Comments _____

CAMPAIGN BROCHURE TEXT

The campaign brochure is probably your most important piece of literature. The brochure can take many forms and be any length. Make it easy on the eye, both in appearance and content. Concentrate on the most important issues only. Collect brochures from previous campaigns in your town and from other cities and towns to help you develop your design. Below are some suggestions to get you thinking.

What are the benefits?

- A modern facility will improve learning opportunities.
- Improved safety and health for our children—if our existing school were built today, it would not meet fire, ventilation, and safety codes.
- The new school design meets the federal regulations for handicapped/ universal access. People who have difficulty walking and climbing stairs will be able to attend and enjoy school programs and activities.
- A new school is a positive attraction for new businesses and residents. Some former and prospective residents have chosen other towns with more modern school facilities.

Why now?

- If not now, *when?* No major improvements have been made to the elementary school since 1955.
- District 7 has had no bonded debt for over ten years.
- Interest rates are low, but they are slowly rising. If we continue to wait, the cost will only increase.
- The cost of operating and maintaining the old school is high, and it will increase.
- The longer we wait, the less facility we will be able to buy for our money.

What will we get for our money?

- A new modern, no frills school, with all students under one roof.
- A single-level building that meets all fire, safety, and universal access laws.
- Separate dining area so gym facilities can be used for physical education. The gym will be used all day for classes and other learning activities.

- Off-street student drop off and parking, improving safety for our young citizens.
- Classrooms of adequate size, each with space for computer instruction.
- The bond can be used only to build a new school. The money cannot be used for school maintenance, salaries, or supplies.

What will it cost?

- The cost of the bond is $4,735,000 and will have an estimated interest rate of 6.5 percent. It will be retired over a 20-year period.
- The present valuation of district X is estimated to be $114,211,384.
- The bond fund levy required to make the annual payments will be 36.5 cents per $100 of valuation.
- The total school levy in 1998 was $1.79. With the new school, the total school levy would be $1.58, using the 1994–1995 school levy.
- This levy will continue to be reduced if the district's valuation increases.
- The bond interest rate is fixed and cannot increase. After five years the bond may be refinanced if interest rates are lower.
- The bond issue will include all costs related to this project: new construction, site development, parking, demolition of the old school, and professional fees.

The Result

- A school with room to grow, with adequate classroom size for efficient, comfortable learning and teaching.
- Lower maintenance and operating costs owing to modern construction and equipment and state-of-the-art utilities and insulation.
- Safe and efficient flow-through access from 4th and 7th Streets.
- Adequate water and sewer facilities and connections included in the bond price.
- A flexible building plan designed for easy expansion as the student population grows. No more need for portable classrooms!

Frequently Asked Questions

Why build new instead of renovating the old school? The old school and its additions are between 45 and 72 years old. Because of their age, the buildings are difficult and expensive to maintain and repair. The classrooms do not lend themselves to modern teaching methods (inadequate wiring, small classroom size, acoustical problems). We need to improve our programs in math, science, computers, and physical education. The old buildings are simply not up to the task. To upgrade the old structures to comply with new regulations regarding health, safety, and handicapped access will be nearly impossible and extremely expensive. The old buildings will only cost more in upgrades. Our wisest long-term investment would be to build anew.

Is it true air conditioning will be included in this project? Air conditioning is included as part of the heating system. Almost all modern heating and ventilation systems include air conditioning. The cost of installing air conditioning will be a minimal part of this project.

Who decided what is needed? A school facilities study was commissioned by the school board in (year). Three additional studies conducted by (names and dates) verified the proposed needs. The K.I.D.S. Committee recently conducted a survey of district voters in which 74 percent supported school improvement. Many of the citizens' suggestions were included in this proposal.

After bond approval, how soon will the buildings be built? The architect projects a 22-month construction period. All work should be completed by the start of the (year–year) school year.

Conclusion Statements

Past generations paid for our present facilities. Now it is our turn. After us, future generations will take their turn. So that quality education continues, please support the school bond initiative on (date). Our goal must be to keep students and their educational needs as the focus of this issue. Each individual may find parts of the proposal that he does not like, but to reach our goal, we must compromise. Keep foremost in mind the benefits to our young citizens, our community, and our future.

Senior Exemption

(If such a law exists in your state, be sure to remind seniors of it. Most may see no increase in their property tax assessment, thereby removing a major reason to oppose the bond.)

The Homestead Exemption law provides a 100 percent property tax exemption on homes with an actual value of up to $35,000. This exemption applies if the home is owned and occupied by a person 65 years old with an adjusted federal gross income tax of $10,400 or less. Please contact John Taxman, County Assessor, at 432-6789 for details.

How Will This Affect Me?

(Here are some ideas for your money section of the brochure. Try to include basic cost analysis without belaboring the issue too much. Try to relate the cost to everyday minor expenses.)

If your property is assessed . . .   Your tax will be . . .

	$45,000	25 cents per day $7.60 per month $91.25 per year
	$65,000	65 cents per day $19.50 per month $234 per year
	$85,000	85 cents per day $25.50 per month $306 per year

Final Touches

An architect's drawing and/or floor plan of the new or renovated building or addition adds to the brochure and helps to show people what they will be getting for their tax dollars.

Also, be sure to note on the brochure that it was created by the committee and paid for with private donations.

Bibliography

Bly, Robert W. 1990. *The Copywriter's Handbook: A Step-by-Step Guide to Writing Copy That Sells.* New York: Henry Holt & Co.

Etheredge, Forest D. 1989. *School Boards and the Ballot Box: How to Win Elections for Your Schools and Yourself.* Alexandria, Va.: National School Boards Association.

Holt, Carleton Roland. 1993. "Factors Affecting the Outcomes of School Bond Elections in South Dakota." Ph.D diss., University of South Dakota.

Ough, Michael L. 1991. "A Study of Selected Factors Affecting Voter Behavior in Nebraska School Bond Elections." Ph.D diss., University of Nebraska, Lincoln.

Technical Assistance Research Program. 1999. *Basic Facts on Customer Complaint Behavior and the Impact of Service on the Bottom Line.* Special report prepared by John Goodman. Arlington, Va. http://www.e-satisfy.com/pdf/basicfacts.pdf.

U.S. Bureau of the Census. 2000. *America's Families and Living Arrangements: Population Characteristics.* Special report prepared by Jason Fields and Lynne M. Casper. Washington, D.C. http://www.census.gov/prod/2001pubs/p20-537pdf.

U.S. Department of Education. 2001. *Record Enrollments at Elementary and Secondary Schools, Colleges, and Universities Expected This Fall.* Press release. Washington, D.C. http://www.ed.gov/PressReleases/08-2001/08162001.html.

———. 2000. *Record School Enrollments, Again, As Baby Boom Echo Extends Into the Future.* Press release. Washington, D.C. http://www.ed.gov/PressReleases/08-2000/0821.html.

U.S. General Accounting Office. 2000. *School Facilities: Construction Expenditures Have Grown Significantly in Recent Years.* GAO/HEHS-00-41. A special report prepared at the request of the U.S. House of Representatives. Washington, D.C. http://www.gao.gov/nav/html.

Index

About the Author

Raised in California, **Cheryl M. Conrod** has lived in most of the western states. She has been a journalist, park ranger, furniture builder, photographer, substitute teacher, and freelance writer. She currently teaches English as a second language and tutors writing skills at New Mexico State University at Alamogordo, New Mexico, where she lives with her husband Bill and son DJ.